ART DECO

THE EUROPEAN STYLE

ART DECO

THE EUROPEAN STYLE

SARAH MORGAN

DORSET PRESS

This edition published 1990 by
Dorset Press
A division of Marboro Books Corp.
by arrangement with Brompton Books Corp.

Produced by
Brompton Books Corp.
15 Sherwood Place
Greenwich, CT 06830

ISBN 0-88029-485-X

Printed in Hong Kong

Page 1: This clock by Van Cleef and Arpels, 1926, is designed in the form of a Japanese temple portico; the signs of the zodiac replace numerals.

Page 2: *The Flame Dancer* by Ferdinand Preiss, cold-painted bronze and ivory, c. 1930, is typical of his later, more contemporary style and illustrates the high quality of his ivory carving.

CONTENTS

INTRODUCTION

Opposite: Gerrit Rietveld's Red-Blue chair, c. 1917, reflects the emphasis laid on straight lines and primary colors by the Dutch De Stijl movement, which adopted an intellectual approach to design and rejected ornamentation.

Art Deco is not a clearly defined movement; the term covers a period in the history of the decorative arts (including a portion of the fine arts), a style which developed from just prior to World War I and which lasted on into the 1930s, though not in quite the same form.

Art Deco began as a specifically French or even Parisian creation and remained essentially a French style. Yet many designers elsewhere in Europe were influenced by French design and worked in the same, or a similar, idiom. Whether or not a piece displays French influence does not always define its claim to be called a work of Art Deco. Important variants of Art Deco were created in countries other than France, while some designers based their designs less obviously on the French style but still produced work that captured that same spirit. With hindsight a remarkable similarity of theme and style can be detected in work produced throughout Europe and America in the interwar period.

Some of the French designers of Art Deco labeled their work '*style moderne*', but no really comprehensive general term existed to cover the various manifestations of the style until the 1960s. The phrase is derived from the title of the Exposition des Arts Decoratifs et Industriels, which was held in Paris in 1925 and was an important landmark in the history of Art Deco.

The early years of the twentieth century, known as the Edwardian era in England and the *belle époque* in France, represent rather the last moments of an extended nineteenth century than the beginnings of a new one, despite the promise of ever-increasing technological advancement. For the turn of the century launched Europe into a second Industrial Revolution. Cars began to fill the streets, buses and taxis were becoming motorized, and the railway and underground networks were expanding. Electricity and central heating were gradually entering homes, as were the telephone, the wireless and the gramophone. The capitalist economy was booming, and until World War I only a handful of socialists spoke of its imminent collapse. The bourgeoisie hardly felt the threat of socialism; pre-war Europe was in a very confident state of mind.

Yet society was on the brink of radical change, and the symptoms of that change were becoming increasingly evident. The new and more efficient modes of transport, the advances in communication, the growth of the media and the changes taking place in the home were all harbingers of the new age, signaling the beginnings of a social upheaval that would lead among other things to the emancipation of women and improved conditions for the lower classes. As if fearful of the future, however, the wealthy upper classes studiously ignored the changes that were taking place, and resolved instead to prolong the past with a kind of mad intent, holding fast to the rigid class structure as if to a sinking ship.

As far as the arts are concerned, they were far ahead in predicting (and instrumenting) change. The turn of the century marks the point at which the Modern movement in the fine arts and literature was born. It is important to remember that this revolution took place not during the war or immediately after, but some years before. In 1905 the Fauves burst on the

Right: Süe et Mare's *Parfums d'Orsay* shopfront, c. 1925; Parisian high style Deco was in many ways epitomized by the work of Süe et Mare.

scene with their brilliant color effects and their exaggeration of form and perspective. It was the beginning of the break with naturalism and the move towards abstraction.

The style that preceded Art Deco in the history of the decorative arts was Art Nouveau, which developed in the 1880s and reached maturity at the turn of the century. This was something of a compromise between advancement and the deliberate refusal to face the future that was characteristic of its epoque. It was modern in the sense that it sought to break with tradition, and the historical plagiarism that dominated the arts through the nineteenth century, and to establish a new decorative vocabulary that could be applied almost universally. On the other hand it was retrogressive in the sense that its exponents did little to make it available to anyone but the very wealthy or to adapt it to the machine, but instead raised the designer-craftsman to the status of artist and concentrated on the production of handcrafted *pièces uniques* for an elite clientele. The Paris exhibition of 1900 marked the demise of Art Nouveau as a fashionable style, though it was popularized in a degraded form until well into the 1920s.

In retrospect, the graceful lines and delicate tones of Art Nouveau, although for a while considered quite avant-garde, seem to reflect the decadence of the old world and therefore seem doomed to die the same death. It is significant that Art Deco, though it owes much to Art Nouveau, scarcely reproduces those sinuous lines. By and large the change is abrupt; straight lines and geometrical forms take the place of those indulgent meandering curves, and in its mature style Art Deco's boldness, dynamism and compact forms are a complete antithesis to Art Nouveau.

Art Deco developed in response to the general pressure to adapt to the modern world and, specifically, was a stage in an already burgeoning revolution in the decorative arts. As the pace of change accelerated in the early twentieth century, it became clear that the lingering traces of the previous era needed to be eradicated and the environment to be redesigned. Three countries, France, Austria and Germany, came to the fore in the search for a suitably modern decorative idiom.

Art Nouveau had begun as a serious attempt to integrate art into social life and to establish a new style by looking to nature, but it quickly degenerated into a celebration of decoration for its own sake. In England the architect Charles Francis Annesley Voysey influenced a movement opposed to Art Nouveau and shortly afterwards in Vienna the architect Otto Wagner, inspired by the work of Charles Rennie Mackintosh, began to advocate the adoption of a new form of design that abolished curves and was based on geometrical forms. Charles Rennie Mackintosh adapted Art Nouveau in an individualistic fashion and tamed the flamboyant curves, introducing them into a geometrical play of verticals, horizontals and spatial volumes. His work used ornament to set off a more severe, sober and functional style and was an important precursor of Art Deco.

Left: Wells Coates 'AD65' radio for Ecko, 1933. Designers of mass-produced objects such as fridges, radios, cameras and clocks took their inspiration from Deco.

Below: Cover design by Aubrey Beardsley for *The Yellow Book*. Beardsley's sinuous graphic style and decadent manner was as great an influence on Deco designers as on the masters of Art Nouveau before them.

Right: Josef Hoffmann's footed silver dish with cover, 1902. Hoffmann was more severe and rigorous in his tastes than other members of the Vienna Secession, employing a strict geometry in his designs for furniture and metalwork.

Far right: Charles Rennie Mackintosh's armchair with colored glass insets, 1904, is an example of his tamed and geometrical Art Nouveau style.

As a result of Wagner's teaching a group of artists was formed in Vienna who broke away from the Academy and set themselves up as the Vienna Secession. Their common resolve was to abolish Art Nouveau and replace it with something more rigorous and modern, and they were greatly influenced by the work of Mackintosh and the English Arts and Crafts movement with its focus on craft production (a reaction to the shoddy industrialized goods produced in the nineteenth century). The lead-

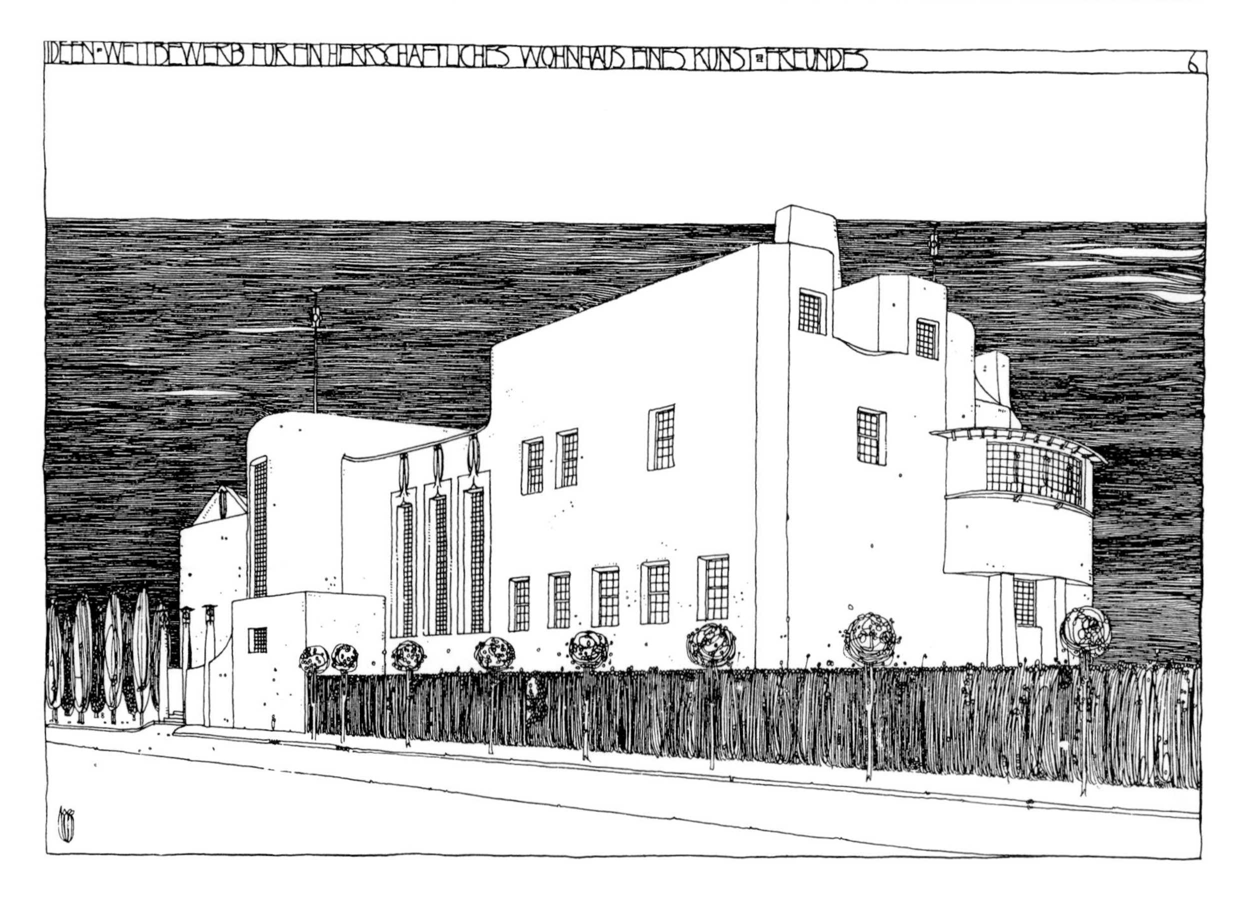

Right: Charles Rennie Mackintosh's sketch for a 'House for a Lover of the Arts', 1901. Notice the similarity to the Palais Stoclet (right), particularly in the block forms and the decorative grouping of windows.

ing members of the Secession were the architect-cum-designers Josef Hoffmann and Josef Maria Olbrich and the designer Koloman Moser. The general focus was on craftsmanship and industrial techniques were applied only rarely; this was essentially an expensive style that depended on rich patrons. Olbrich built the Secession headquarters in 1897-98; its blocked forms and stylized decoration, applied not indiscriminately but in an ordered and restrained manner, make it an important forerunner of Art Deco.

In 1903 the Wiener Werkstätte was established, under the joint direction of Hoffmann and Moser, to manufacture and sell the designs of the Secession artists. Their first important commission was the magnificent Palais Stoclet in Brussels, built for a Belgian coal magnate, which was begun in 1905 but not finished until 1911. Hoffman designed the building and numerous Werkstätte artists collaborated on its decoration. From the cutlery to the mosaic murals in the dining room, which were designed by Gustav Klimt, an astonishing homogeneity was achieved, an aspect of Austrian design that particularly impressed French and German designers. Another feature of the design throughout the building was the use of luxurious materials and the combination of floral and geometrical motifs and patterns. These elements too were absorbed into Art Deco, although rendered more lightly and gracefully by French designers.

Meanwhile, still in Austria, there existed a more radical movement headed by the architect Adolf Loos, a movement that for aesthetic

Above: Josef Maria Olbrich's Vienna Secession building, 1897-8, an important forerunner of Art Deco.

Left: The Palais Stoclet in Brussels, 1905-11, designed by Josef Hoffmann, the first major Wiener Werkstätte commission.

and ideological reasons sought to abolish ornament altogether. His ideas had more in common with the emergent German style.

At the time when the Vienna Secession was becoming established, Germany had a more pressing reason for finding a suitable modern style that could be applied to everyday objects and furnishings; it sought a foothold in the increasingly competitive European market. Through the initiative and encouragement of the government and the efforts of Hermann Muthesius, who headed the project, an organization named the Deutsche Werkbund was founded in 1907 whose members were both artists and industrialists. Their goal was to promote the application of new design techniques in industry, and so to improve the standard of manufactured goods. The Werkbund became the first organization to recognize the potential of the machine and the importance of industrialization in the new century. Muthesius made a lengthy study of English design and decided that the new style, like the work of the Werkstätte, should be based on the sober and functional forms of the English Arts and Crafts movement and the work of Charles Rennie Mackintosh, yet without the focus on the manual production of goods. He stressed the importance of maintaining a simple and unified style that was identifiably German.

Below: This set of glassware designed by Adolf Loos is an example of the extreme simplicity of Modernist design.

Peter Behrens was a founder member of the Werkbund and successfully applied its tenets in industrial design and packaging, notably in his work for the company AEG. Later, as director of the arts and crafts school in Düsseldorf, he set an important precedent in his reform and modernization of art education.

As a result of the success of the Werkbund, a style began to emerge in Germany in the first decade of the twentieth century that was simple, smart and distinctly modern. The French were rather taken aback, when the Deutsche Werkbund exhibited a few interiors at the 1910 Salon d'Automne, to discover that the Germans had developed a strong new decorative idiom while they had been casting about for styles to revive as Art Nouveau waned. They had to admit its success, and much of the change that then took place in the decorative arts in Paris can be attributed to the influence of German design at this exhibition.

Although Art Deco appeared to reject Art Nouveau wholeheartedly, it in fact retained many of the characteristics of its predecessor. Its attempts to be modern were half-hearted and it remained very much an expensive, hand-crafted luxury. It was almost as if the purpose of both styles was to exclude the machine by requiring elaborate tasks that only a craftsman could perform; Art Nouveau with its intricate carving, Art Deco with its complicated veneers and its emphasis on exquisite cabinetry. As a result decoration remained a major feature of the new style and the decorative fantasy world of flowers, women and fauna, which was partly inherited from Art Nouveau and partly from traditional classical-inspired design, was adapted and stylized in keeping with the new idiom. It is significant that a number of designers who had worked in the Art Nouveau style became early exponents of Art Deco; René Lalique, Maurice Dufrène, Paul Follot and Léon-Albert Jallot among others. From the beginning Art Deco was characterized by its likeness to Art Nouveau. While it responded to the pioneering work of the Werkstätte and the Werkbund in its search for a modern idiom that could be applied to all areas of design and its rejection of the outmoded curves and excesses of Art Nouveau, its emphasis on the manual production of goods and distrust of the machine excluded it from the avant-garde movements that were forming in northern Europe. Art Deco always represented a more conservative alternative to the extreme changes in design and production proposed by more radical groups.

Designers in Paris began to cast about for ways of interpreting the new developments in Germany and Austria in a French manner. For

Left: Two celebrities of the Deco period: Paul Poiret and Josephine Baker at a party *chez* Poiret.

it was important that France should uphold its traditional reputation for innovation and excellence in the arts and design and, on a more practical level, that she should combat the influx of foreign manufactured goods. A Société des Artistes Décorateurs had been in existence since 1901 and was active in organizing regular exhibitions. In 1903 the Salon d'Automne was founded, where designers and decorators were encouraged to exhibit alongside fine artists. This was a period when painters, sculptors and architects were becoming increasingly involved with design and the decorative arts.

Although some designers looked to sources such as traditional French provincial furniture for inspiration, the mainstream continued to draw on the styles of the late eighteenth century. The neoclassical style adapted well to the increasing urge to simplify forms; Jacques-Emile Ruhlmann was among its chief exponents. From early on his work was an absolutely simple, pared-down interpretation of neoclassical forms, and the high standard of craftsmanship that he maintained was also inspired by eighteenth-century craftsmen.

Art Deco was largely based on this neoclassical revival but it was also a very promiscuous style, borrowing arbitrarily from a variety of sources, particularly Oriental and Middle Eastern art forms. The arrival of Diaghilev's Ballets Russes company in Paris in 1909 triggered a fascination with these foreign sources and struck a note that resounded through the ensuing years, one of sexual liberation, gaiety and creative vigor. The Parisian public was immediately enchanted by the vivid color, the decorative exuberance of the sets and the sensuous nature of the dancing. The preoccupation of the Ballets Russes with Persian and Oriental themes, so exquisitely and lavishly rendered in the sets and costumes of Léon Bakst, rapidly became absorbed into French design. The couturier Paul Poiret, arbiter of taste to the new epoque, was responsible for introducing these new elements into women's fashion. Under his influence ladies donned turbans sprouting extravagant plumes, and loose jewel-colored gowns in satins or heavy brocades that wrapped and draped.

Poiret was a flamboyant character and enormously influential in establishing the new decorative mood. He applied himself to the creation of a new style of furnishing and interior design. Inspired by the Werkbund exhibits at the Salon d'Automne of 1910 and aware that France needed to reassert herself quickly in the field of design, Poiret visited Germany and Austria where he met designers, scrutinized their work and absorbed their ideas. He was full of admiration for what he saw, but disagreed with the methods of training young artists and the way that pupils were

Below: Chinese vase of the Sung dynasty, twelfth to thirteenth century. The restrained elegance of Oriental design influenced all disciplines, but was particularly apparent in the field of ceramics. Compare this vase to those of Lenoble and Decoeur.

Right: Painted wooden cabinet by Otto Prutscher, c. 1910. Prutscher was a member of the Vienna Secession, working in a simple, less rigidly geometric style than that of Hoffmann.

forced to adhere to an established style. He resolved to help create a new French idiom that did not suppress individuality but was fresh and spontaneous. When he returned to Paris in 1911 he set up the Atelier Martine (which he named after one of his daughters). Young, working-class girls were encouraged to sketch and paint from nature instinctively and with minimal tuition. The best results were made up into repeating fabric designs and rugs and were used for furnishing and fashion. The Atelier also manufactured furniture and provided an interior design service. One of the aspects of German and Viennese design which had particularly appealed to Poiret and many other French designers was the harmony and coherence that was achieved in their interiors. French designers sought to emulate this homogeneity, hence the emphasis placed on the *ensemble* (the total design of an interior) and the *ensemblier* (its designer).

Martine furniture was clearly influenced by Werkstätte work, but was less severe in style. Interior schemes were equally inspired by the sumptuous exoticism of the Ballets Russes sets. The simplicity of the furniture was offset by gay colored fabrics, wallpapers and rugs, and heaps of bolsters and cushions in luxuriant satiny fabrics. The style Poiret propagated was a charming blend of naïvety and sophistication. This combination was particularly evident in objects and furniture whose design was based on primitive or early art forms, but made sleek and urbane through stylization, intricate craftsmanship and the use of lavish materials. This became an important feature of Art Deco, as did the idea that the simple and sometimes severe furniture designs of Art Deco should be set in a richly patterned context. Even when furniture was pared down to the simplest tubular steel and plain upholstery, a brightly colored carpet or patterned wallpaper enlivened the setting.

Below: Nijinsky as the negro slave in *Schéhérazade*, 1910, by George Barbier. The Ballets Russes was a major influence on early Art Deco.

The craze for things exotic and eastern begun by the Ballets Russes came at a time when designers were avid for new ideas and motifs from outside the sphere of French historical styles. New influences were quickly absorbed into the Art Deco vernacular. The restraint and elegance of Oriental design and the high standard of craftsmanship were much admired, and inspired the light mannered quality and elegance of Art Deco. The Oriental art of lacquerwork was incorporated into the Art Deco repertoire early on by artists such as Jean Dunand and Eileen Gray. Its smart glossy finish and its versatility – it could be absolutely plain or highly decorative – made lacquer one of the single most popular materials of this period, and it was applied almost universally; to screens and sofas, vases and jewelry, and even to fabrics.

The arts of ancient and primitive civilizations provided Deco with a rich source of motifs and decorative themes. An enthusiasm for African art filtered through from Cubism, and coincided with the fascination with Negro culture that spread across Europe following the arrival of the black jazz musicians from America. The highlight of this influx was the sensational cabaret artiste Josephine Baker, who was propelled to stardom when she was barely twenty, wearing only a string of bananas. The colonial exhibitions that were held in Paris in 1922 and 1931 also helped to familiarize designers and public alike with African art.

In 1922 the tomb of Tutankhamun was discovered and there followed a frenzy of Egyptianizing. Jewelry, handbags, cigarette cases, furniture and even buildings were adorned with, often implausible, Egyptian-style motifs. The best designers studied the Egyptian treasures carefully, and were equally careful to extract whatever elements of Egyptian design were best adapted to their work. Also influential on design, and particularly on Art Deco architecture, were the Mayan and Aztec civilizations of Pre-Columbian America.

It was not uncommon for designers to create fantastical, hybrid styles that combined elements of many ancient and archaic art forms. It is important to recognize that by and large Art Deco designers did not copy slavishly from these sources. There were no scholarly 'quotes'. What these art forms offered was an invaluable source of abstract, geometrical or figurative imagery. As Art Deco designers began to respond to the changes taking place in the arts, and the pressure to 'modernize' grew stronger, the influence of this source material provided a means by which Art Deco could modernize itself without sacrificing its decorative element.

Of all the avant-garde art movements that came into being in the early twentieth century – and most exercised an influence of some sort on Art Deco design – Cubism was the most important for the early development of Art Deco. 1907, the year when Picasso finished painting *Les Demoiselles d'Avignon*, marks the birth of Cubism; Picasso drew widely on influences such as archaic and African sculpture and Egyptian art, as he sought to break with tradition and devise a new means of expression in painting. *Les Demoiselles* heralds an important move away from realism and toward abstraction.

Picasso and Braque developed Cubism from its infancy, creating an art which sought to examine three-dimensional form and the nature of representation. Forms were fragmented, simplified and abstracted, and traditional perspective was abandoned in favor of a multiple-viewpoint perspective. The influence

Above: Russian peasant costume designed by Natalia Goncharova for the Ballets Russes production of *Le Coq d'Or*, 1914.

Left: Bed of the Divine Cow from the tomb of Tutankhamun, c. 1350 BC; stylized animal motifs borrowed from pieces such as this were incorporated into Deco design.

Above: A seventeenth-century Japanese Sutra lacquered storage box with lotus petal design. The decorative quality and sleek aspect of Oriental lacquerwork was greatly admired by Deco designers.

of Cubism quickly spread through the arts, and became absorbed into the decorative arts too – the emergent Art Deco. Art Deco designers adopted superficial aspects of Cubism, incorporating its angular, faceted quality into their stylistic vocabulary and using a 'Cubist' treatment of form to update motifs. This angularizing and faceting was a means of disciplining and homogenizing all the disparate elements of Art Deco. In its later phase, abstract designs of interlocking geometrical forms were applied as ornament and the Synthetic Cubist experiments with collage became incorporated into design in the tendency to juxtapose different materials.

When Art Deco first came into being before World War I, an atmosphere of excitement and innovation was bubbling to the surface all over Europe and particularly in Paris, where new revolutions in the arts were constantly brewing. From America came jazz musicians, night clubs and tales of the towering constructions being erected in New York. When the war came it left everyone a little subdued, but nothing could really halt the march toward modernity. In many ways the urge to forget its horrors and losses drove society on at an even greater pace. Youth was adulated, and women were liberated. Style and lifestyle are intimately related and early Art Deco reflected the light-hearted, furious enjoyment of life. It was the Jazz Age, the Roaring Twenties, *Les Années Folles*, as it was variously styled; a time of cars, cabarets, cocktails and flappers.

The 1920s were a time of liberation in many senses, and were notoriously sexually permissive. The naked female image abounded as a decorative motif and as a theme for painting and sculpture, offering an opportunity to indulge in a little eroticism, but also a potent symbol of modernity. The flapper girl with short hair and bared limbs stood for the new age. It was in this period, too, that advertisers began to recognize the advantages of using the image of the liberated, provocative, modern young woman to attract potential buyers.

After the war a new class of patron began to come to the fore, ousting the old *fin-de-siècle* aristocracy which was rapidly declining in power and wealth. The post-war spending spree that these *nouveaux-riches* embarked upon gave a special impetus to the new style. The luxury products of Art Deco became the emblems or status symbols of this new aristocracy. Under their patronage Art Deco became a style that reflected the new wealth, an elitist style that only the very rich could afford.

The extravagant lifestyle of the rich was epitomized in the great ocean liners that journeyed back and forth between Europe and America. In this period they were larger and faster than ever before, combining the style and extravagance of the old world with the technology, speed and comfort of the new. Under French influence, they were increasingly conceived as showcases of national design. The first luxury French vessels were launched in the early 1920s, culminating in the magnificent *Normandie* which made her maiden voyage in 1935. A tenth of the total cost of the ship was reputedly spent on interior decoration; most of the major designers of the period collaborated on its decoration.

From its rather hesitant beginnings Art Deco soon became a coherent and easily recognizable style, embracing all branches of the decorative arts. This was partly due to the emphasis placed on collaboration and achieving a unity of design in an *ensemble*, and partly also to the interdisciplinary skills of its practitioners. In no other period had artists been so versatile, acquiring skills in a whole range of crafts and disciplines and thus helping to spread the new style.

The establishment of large companies offering Art Deco furnishings and interior design schemes did much to publicize and consolidate the style. Ruhlmann set up his company in 1919 and in the same year Louis Süe and André Mare founded their Compagnie des Arts Français, both aiming to provide a complete decorating service. The growing number of magazines concerned with design and decorating also helped to promote and spread the style.

An important homogenizing influence on Art Deco was the 1925 Paris Exposition. It was 18 years in the planning, and the idea of presenting a coherent front to the rest of Europe must constantly have been in the minds of its organizers and contributers. It was particularly important in the development of Art Deco abroad, influencing design throughout Europe and in America.

At the same time it is important not to overemphasize the unity and rigidity of the style. The Paris Exposition is generally agreed to

Left: Bed-sitting room designed by Bauhaus artists Walter Gropius and Marcel Breuer, 1926-27; the spare Bauhaus style influenced the modernistic phase of Art Deco.

mark the demise of the floral, elaborate and highly patterned style based on traditional French design which is best described as 'high style' Art Deco. This gave way to a mature phase dominated by the influence of Modernism, which can be labeled 'modernistic' Art Deco. The two phases are clearly closely related, however; Art Deco, though an evolving style, continued to be decorative, fashionable and eclectic and by and large it also retained its wealthy patrons.

The patronage of the great Parisian couturier Jacques Doucet helped to consolidate a middle style that bridged the gap between the decorative high style of Deco and its modernistic phase. In 1912 Doucet sold his fine collection of eighteenth-century furniture and art, in order to devote himself to the patronage of contemporary artists. By the mid-1920s he had replaced his old collection with a new one: paintings by Picasso, Braque, Matisse, Derain and the Douanier Rousseau among others, and sculpture by Brancusi and Zadkine. He had also assembled a considerable collection of African tribal art. These were housed in a new apartment at 46 Avenue du Bois. The apartment was furnished by a group of designers who worked in a remarkably coherent style and were undoubtedly influenced by Doucet's own tastes; their strong, simple and geometrical designs were inspired by Cubism as well as African and (to a lesser extent) Oriental art.

Deco's modernistic phase was also greatly influenced by the radical art movements such as De Stijl, Futurism, the Bauhaus and Constructivism. The Dutch De Stijl group was an active force in the interwar period. Its theories

Below: *Camouflaged Ships in Dry Dock – Liverpool*, 1918, by Edward Wadsworth. He was a founder member of the British Vorticist group, which inspired a stark and dramatic decorative style.

Right: AM Cassandre's poster for the *Atlantique* liner, 1931, epitomizes the luxury of Art Deco.

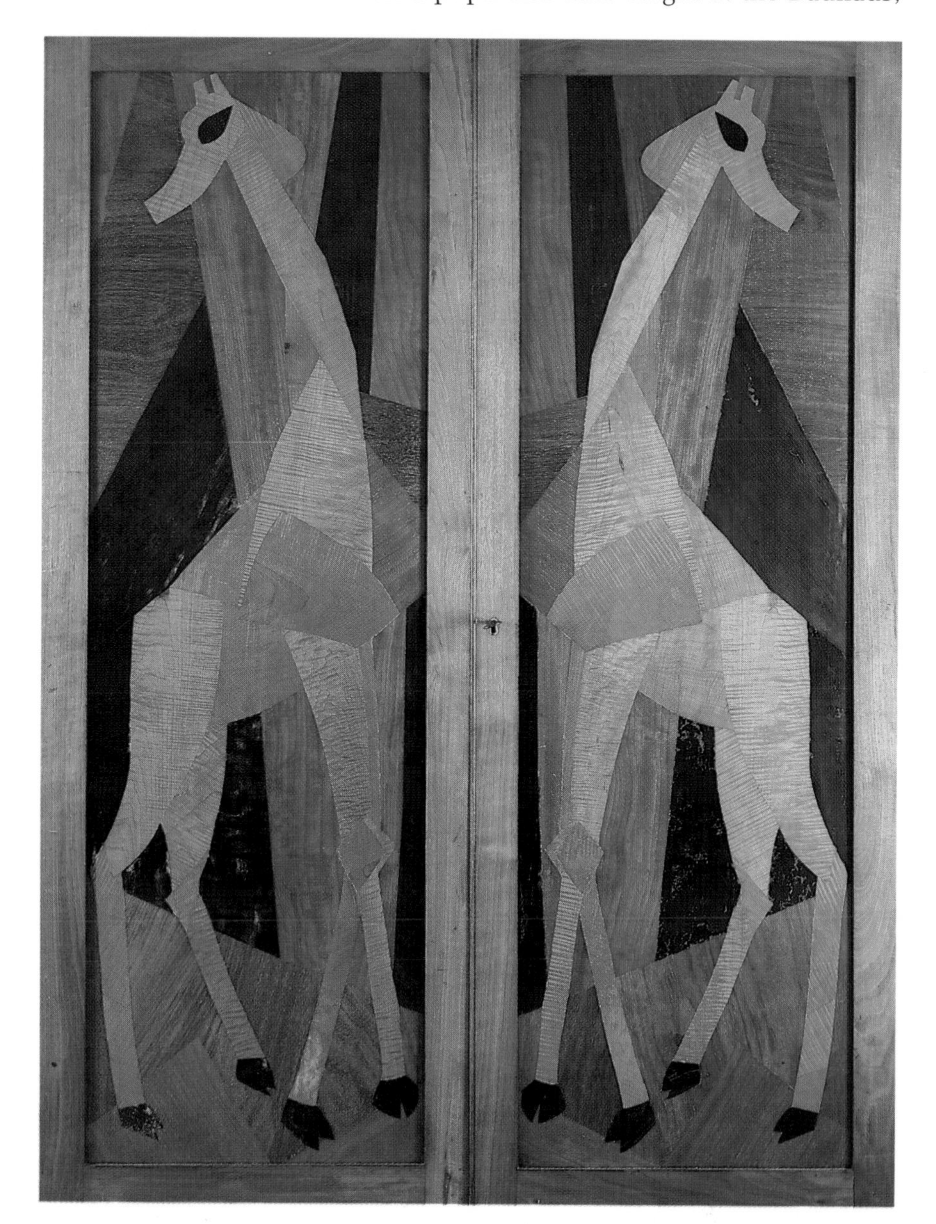

Below: Marquetry cupboard doors, c. 1914, by Roger Fry for the Omega workshops. Fry was one of the first in England to apply Cubist theories to the decorative arts.

were influenced both by Cubism and by Neoplatonist philosophy, and it aspired to utopian ideals concerning the unification of art and life. The members of De Stijl developed an entirely abstract or non-objective art that was based on the interplay of horizontals and verticals. Color was restricted to the three primaries, red, blue and yellow, and was used to accent the arrangement of planes in space. The architect Gerrit Rietveld applied their theories to the design of furniture and then to architecture. De Stijl work was stark, simple and functional, although functionalism remained secondary to the resolution of spatial problems.

The Bauhaus art school was set up by Walter Gropius in Weimar in 1919. The early years of its existence were devoted to Expressionism, but the arrival of the De Stijl artist Van Doesburg in 1921 helped to bring about considerable changes in its teaching and theories. He set about preaching the ideas of De Stijl to the Bauhaus and its pupils and, although there was some resistance at first, the influence was quickly absorbed. Marcel Breuer, who was then a pupil and later taught at the Bauhaus, was particularly receptive to the influence of De Stijl. In 1922 the Russian Constructivist László Moholy-Nagy was appointed to the staff of the Bauhaus and introduced a further influence into the mix. He helped to eradicate the last traces of the Expressionist focus on craftsmanship and the notion of art as a spiritual revelation, and emphasized instead the relationship of art and industry, and the rational use of techniques and materials. The new Bauhaus style was geared for industry and bound up with revolutionary socialist theories, and was characterized by simple geometrical shapes, uniform areas of pure color and a complete absence of ornament. This Bauhaus style was particularly apparent from 1925, the year of the school's move to Dessau. The progressive atmosphere of the school nurtured great talents who helped to revolutionize the tools of everyday living and considerably influenced twentieth-century design. The Bauhaus is particularly famous for its pioneering of metal furniture design, which was to become one of the basic features of the modernistic Deco interior. It went on producing its innovative designs until the Nazis closed the school in 1933.

Intimately connected with developments at the Bauhaus was the Swiss architect Le Corbusier, who had worked for a time under Peter Behrens. His Esprit Nouveau pavilion designed for the 1925 Paris Exposition was clearly influenced by the Bauhaus and De Stijl. Le Corbusier deplored the prevailing obsession with ornament, and the starkness of his pavilion was in part a reaction against it.

The general aim of these pioneering Modernists was to promote change in the field of design and architecture by establishing exemplary models for furnishing, household objects and buildings which were functional and cheap to manufacture. Good design had to become available to people of all classes. They envisaged a time when the modern proletariat would inhabit high-rise blocks of white concrete and glass in apartments that were spacious, light and hygienic.

Left: Advertisement for the Delahaye motor car, c. 1930; note the streamlined design of the bodywork.

Below: Pablo Picasso: *Les Demoiselles d'Avignon*, 1907, a seminal Cubist work.

Right: The Coca-Cola bottling company plant in Los Angeles, 1936 (Robert V Derrah, architect), a good example of American streamlined Deco.

Toward the mid-1920s the rich decorative quality of the high style began to pall, and to give way to a more sober style. Designers began to respond to the Modernist developments, paring down forms and abolishing superfluous ornament. But their work was still invested with a Deco spirit; they continued to design for a rich elite, to use rare and luxurious materials, and in many respects they still held fast to the ideals of craftsmanship. Their use of abstract patterns and the build-up of forms shows a decorative quality that also distinguishes their work as Art Deco; it seems that designers assimilated the forms but not the doctrine of Modernism. The gloss of lacquer, shiny chrome and highly polished rare wood veneers maintained a chic and exclusive quality. Under the influence of the Bauhaus, craftsmen turned to re-examine the traditions of their craft and to seek decorative possibilities in the materials themselves. Applied ornament gave way to an abstract, decorative play of planes, forms and textured surfaces; floral motifs gave way to bold geometrical ones. In some cases the dividing line between Art Deco and Modernism is indistinct, and there are points at which the two styles converge.

In 1930 a group called the Union des Artistes Modernes was formed, with the intention of actively promoting a more sober style that made use of metal and other modern materials. The founding members came from various decorative disciplines and included Raymond Templier, Hélène Henri, Francis Jourdain, René Herbst and Robert Mallet-Stevens. As early as 1931 their campaigning had become redundant for their aims had by and large been achieved. The mood of frivolity had been sustained throughout the 1920s but was brutally destroyed by the Wall Street stock market crash of 1929 and the ensuing years of economic depression. The mad gaiety of the 1920s gave way to a period of social criticism and introspection, during which the modernistic tendencies of Art Deco were firmly established, decorative pomp and celebration of wealth were finally suppressed, and Bauhaus puritanism began to appeal more strongly.

Futurism inspired an obssession with modernity and the machine. Marinetti's Futurist manifesto, published in France in 1909, declared the need to demolish the past and celebrate in its place all the attributes of the modern world, above all speed and mechanical energy. The Futurists adapted the formal fragmentation of Cubism, seeking to express energy and movement in their work. Their vitality and preoccupation with speed became reflected in much Art Deco design, and Futurist methods of conveying vigor, movement and dynamism were adopted and exploited by Deco artists.

An important variant of modernistic Art Deco was the streamlined style. It is generally associated with American Art Deco, but was adapted to European design partly in response to the Futurist call to glorify speed and the machine. Streamlining exaggerated horizontal features and emphasized smooth curves, and was adopted in the design of cars, buses, trains and airplanes, in architecture, and to some extent in furniture design. It came to be applied to mass-produced objects such as fridges and radios to suggest modernity.

Most other countries of Europe made some attempt to update the decorative arts, inspired by the examples of Germany, Austria and France. Scandinavia was far ahead in developing a simple, cheap and functional style. Swedish glassware was particularly striking, echoing the mood of French Art Deco and evolving along similar lines. Germany developed a variant of the French style, although much heavier and less appealing, alongside the increasingly prevalent Bauhaus style. In Italy a modern style was evolved that was tempered with neoclassicism but showed some French influence, particularly in the area of graphic design. The Werkstätte style continued to dominate Austrian design through the 1920s, growing more floral and folky as it matured.

In England a group of artists known as the Omega group made an early attempt to modernize the decorative arts and, like the French, took their cue from avant-garde painting and particularly Cubism. The resulting style was in some ways comparable to early Deco, in that it was decorative and based on floral and animal designs as well as abstract patterns. In other ways, however, it was very different; furnishings were inexpensive with a deliberately hand-crafted feel. The Omega style had little immediate effect on British decorative arts; until the 1930s British design was still steeped in Arts and Crafts and reproduction styles. In the early 1930s Britain woke up to the developments that had been taking place in Europe, and French Deco began to exert a considerable influence. Vorticism, so named because of its intense focal perspective, was an English movement of the pre-war period which developed in response to both Cubism and Futurism; its influence contributed to the evolution of a strong decorative style in England. Like Futurism it was inspired by modern developments in technology, particularly in the fields of photography, engineering and architecture. The two editions of the movement's magazine *Blast* introduced important early innovations to graphic design and typography. Vorticism was also successfully adapted to the abstract patterning of decorative art design.

In Eastern European countries, notably Poland and Czechoslovakia, a style evolved which drew on the influence of Cubism and the decorative Wiener Werkstätte manner but was based on traditional folk styles. Czechoslovakia in particular developed a strongly Cubist style that has much in common with Art Deco.

From being a style created for an elite, Art Deco inevitably became popularized. It was apparent early on that Deco had tremendous selling power in terms of design, packaging and advertising. Many of its exponents were employed by manufacturers and retailers to give their products an extra boost. The profusion of magazines, posters, new shops and galleries meant that the style became familiar to the man on the street and began to filter down to a mass market.

After the Wall Street crash, Art Deco lost many of its important patrons, and manufacturers were forced to look to a less moneyed clientele for their source of revenue. The pared-down forms of modernistic Art Deco were well suited to mass production, being inspired by the industrial Modernist style. Public taste proved to be better disposed toward Art Deco than the austere Modernist style, and the 1930s saw a wealth of cheap goods in materials such as bakelite and chrome which were copies or adaptations of expensive Deco designs.

Left: Bathroom designed for a Cecil B De Mille film of the early 1930s. Hollywood adopted and propagated a more glamorous streamlined version of the modernistic European style.

TOURISME
RENSEIGNE
MENTS DE
TOURISME·
AVIATION·
BILLETS-
DE CHI·DE
FER NAVI
GATION·
1925

1
THE 1925 PARIS EXPOSITION

Opposite: Robert Mallet-Stevens's watercolor of his Tourism pavilion for the 1925 Paris Exposition shows the Modernist influence on later Art Deco.

The idea of holding an international exhibition of the decorative arts was conceived as early as 1907. Eighteen years went by before the exhibition was held – World War I intervened and partly as a result plans were endlessly delayed and rescheduled. The Exposition Internationale des Arts Décoratifs et Industriels Modernes eventually took place in Paris from April to October 1925.

It so happened that the exhibition fixed and focused on an important moment in the development of the decorative arts, and particularly in the evolution of Art Deco, when the high style was on the verge of giving way to the mature and designer's were allowing Modernism to lead them forward. Because of the hostility still felt so keenly after the war, Germany was not invited to participate and the exhibition was deprived of what would have been an important element – a Bauhaus exhibit. Nonetheless Modernism was a strong presence at the exhibition; the Russian and Czechoslovakian avant-garde and minority factions in other countries, including Le Corbusier and his followers, all made uncompromising and controversial statements about design.

The Exposition was an opportunity to publicize, both abroad and at home, the French Art Deco style in its confident maturity. Although designers had exhibited at the Salons over the years, this was their first opportunity to present themselves as exponents of a comprehensive style, embracing all branches of the decorative arts. In general terms it was a point of consolidation but it was also a point of departure, in that it marked the demise of the high Deco style and the spread of French influence through Europe and America.

The exhibition was intended to be entirely modern in character. The regulations of entry were quite insistent on this point and an Admissions Committee was set up to vet entries. America was frightened off by so exacting a requirement and, feeling it had nothing modern to offer, declined to take part.

The text of the 12-volume catalogue of the exhibition asserts definite Modernist sympathies. It advocates machine-age aesthetics praising purity of form, sobriety of decor, the exploitation of new materials. It discusses the state of the decorative arts at the turn of the century and the successful application of a modern style in most areas of the decorative arts. Yet it reflects an attitude that is not completely in tune with the ideals of Modernism. While the production of well designed inexpensive goods is encouraged, it is also made clear that the best design should be reserved for luxury goods.

It would be wrong, however, to assume that the Exposition was all about high fashion furnishings for the very rich. There were all kinds

Below: The Porte d'Honneur, designed by Henri Favier and André Ventre with metalwork by Edgar Brandt, showing the view through the exhibition grounds to the Invalides on the far side of the river.

of pavilions and constructions, some representing the humbler aspects of modern life, from village houses to hostels, schools and churches. Here the exuberance of high Deco was inappropriate, but some of these buildings and interiors successfully incorporated a mild adaptation of the style.

The exhibition was held in the centre of Paris; across the Alexandre III Bridge, along both banks of the River Seine, and stretching up to embrace the Grand Palais. Exhibitors were allotted a site with space to build a pavilion and garden. Since the pavilions were entirely temporary and everything was to be pulled down at the finish, they were built in the cheapest materials; wooden frames and plaster, or concrete.

Thirteen gateways were set up at intervals around the exhibition grounds. These were extraordinary erections, grandiose and fantastic in conception, many of them archetypally high Art Deco in style, with their exaggerated proportions and stereotyped decorative features. The main entrance, the Porte d'Honneur, was designed by Henri Favier and André Ventre and consisted of groups of columns, each one crowned by a stylized pyramidal fountain, stepped back from the main road. The fountain motif was repeated in Edgar Brandt's highly decorative openwork grille which linked each group of columns to the next. With the Grand Palais looming to the left behind the gates and the unbroken vista through to the far end of the exhibition ground, it was a dramatic entrance.

In order to disguise the *fin de siècle* exuberance of the Alexandre III Bridge, Maurice Dufrène designed an awning with Oriental-inspired swagged roofing, walls set with floral relief panels and a shopping mall beneath. Designers who could not afford to exhibit in their own pavilions had shops here.

The French put on a fine show; it must have seemed as though no expense had been spared on the part of the hosts. Everywhere there was some extravagant gesture or gorgeous edifice to dazzle the casual visitor. Fairgrounds were set up, gardens laid out, there were ballets, plays, concerts, fashion shows, fireworks and a thousand other entertainments which were intended to maintain an atmosphere of festivity and lavish hospitality.

At night the spectacular illuminations were a further source of wonderment; in the field of electric lighting nothing so imaginative and on such a grand scale had ever been seen before. Numerous fountains, those *leit-motifs* of Art Deco, were erected and spotlit to enhance the dramatic thrust of the water. Particularly effective was the Lalique fountain in glass; the translucent stem was lit from within and threw a diffused light onto the fine jets of water

Left: Detail of the Porte d'Honneur showing metalwork by Edgar Brandt.

Below: Renè Lalique's illuminated crystal fountain designed for the Paris Exposition.

Right: LH Boileau's Pomone pavilion of Au Marché, showing its massive stepped forms and abundant low-relief decoration.

surrounding it like a mist. At night the Porte de la Concorde by Pierre Patout was transformed into a series of glowing discs hovering above the trees, an effect achieved by lighting only the tops of the columns. The most ostentatious display was the publicity stunt put on by the Citroën company. Colored bulbs were attached to the four sides and up the height of the Eiffel Tower which, when lit, described a series of changing patterns and the company's name and logo.

Paul Poiret, who had been so much a catalyst in the development of Art Deco and had nurtured it in its infancy, was overtaken and left behind by the now nearly mature Deco style. He exhibited three barges which he moored by the Alexandre III Bridge and named *Amours, Délices* and *Orgues*. He had them gutted and redecorated by the Atelier Martine, still in the Wiener Werkstätte-based style he had introduced at least a decade before. *Orgues* was laid out as a night club, with chairs and tables arranged around a dance floor. The expense of this extravagant gesture, and the lack of enthusiasm generated by these rather charming but by now old-fashioned interiors, marked the beginning of Poiret's plummet into financial ruin. He was to die penniless in a charity hospital after many years of obscurity.

Nothing better exemplified the high Art Deco style than the pavilions of the four great department stores, all jostling for attention along the approach to the Invalides. They are in fact better described as caricatures of that style, so fantastic, stagey and over-embellished were they. The opportunity to create exciting, temporary structures was a great incentive to designers to be imaginative and explore the medium. In this case, however, imagination ran to megalomania. The Maîtrise pavilion of Galeries Lafayettes and the Pomone pavilion of Au Bon Marché were massive forms, stepped and faceted to emphasize bulk and height with (particularly in the case of the Pomone pavilion) every available surface decorated in low relief. The façades of both pavilions were dominated by gigantic leaded glass panels in geometrical designs. The Primavera pavilion of the Grands Magasins du Printemps was the most absurd. Like an enormous primitive dwelling-place, it was crowned by a funnel-shaped dome set with glass pebbles. Two pillars flanked a gaping entrance of plain glass. Instead of the usual embellishments of statuettes and relief panels, plants sprouted from the tops of the pillars and around the base of the dome like a frill. The exhibits in these pavilions were an important element in the presentation of Art Deco at the Exposition. They represented the less expensive interpretations of the style and were extremely popular with the public.

Emile-Jacques Ruhlmann, René Lalique and Edgar Brandt made up the great triumvirate that dominated the Exposition, all exhibited widely, all of them were ecstatically praised by public and critics alike and all of them, in their different ways, were leading exponents of high Parisian Deco. Lalique had his own pavilion,

Left: The Primavera pavilion of Printemps, designed by Henri Sauvage and Wybo; the most fantastic and caricatured of the four department store pavilions.

Below: Detail of the Sèvres pavilion designed by the architects Pierre Patout and André Ventre.

decorated with low-relief glass panels, in which he exhibited both large-edition objects and *pièces uniques*; anything and everything that could possibly be cast or blown in glass, from jewelry and scent bottles to floor and wall panels – everything but furniture, which he had not then added to his repertoire. He also designed a dining-room in glass for the Sèvres pavilion, complete with illuminated coffered glass ceiling. Ruhlmann exhibited his work alongside objects by other major Deco designers in his own pavilion, the Hôtel du Collectionneur (home of a patron of the arts), built by Pierre Patout. The simplicity and elegance of his designs, the careful harmonizing of interiors and the sheer luxury of materials caused a sensation. His pavilion was a Pomone type stripped of its decorations and fuss. The forms were more or less the same, but Ruhlmann's building, except for a central relief panel, dared to flaunt its bare concrete. Interest had shifted to the build up of planes, emphasized by subtle horizontal delineation.

Other Art Deco designers prominent at the exhibition were Louis Süe and André Mare, representing high Art Deco at its best – floral but not fussily so, grand, opulent and emphatically based on traditional French styles. They designed and decorated a Museum of Contemporary Art in which they exhibited furnishings designed by members of their company, La Compagnie des Arts Français.

Of the specialist French companies exhibiting decorative wares there were three, all of

Above: Konstantin Melnikov's USSR pavilion was designed in the Russian Constructivist style.

them important and long established, that had successfully integrated the new style into their production, often hiring independent artists to design for them. These were the gold and silversmiths Charles Christofle and the Baccarat glassworks, sharing a pavilion, and the Sèvres company which specialized in porcelain and stoneware.

Perhaps the single most concentratedly Art Deco collaborative effort was the French Embassy prototype, a project realized by the Société des Artistes Décorateurs, and partly funded by the state. Here, the evolving style was quite apparent, alongside the less avant-garde designs of artists like Ruhlmann, André Groult or Jules Leleu. Robert Mallet-Stevens designed the entrance-hall, Francis Jourdain the smoking-room and gymnasium, Pierre Chareau the study-library. In other rooms the collaboration was more intense; the main designers drew others around them to work on every aspect of the interiors. It was an archetypal example of the spread and success of the style.

It would have been apparent to anyone assessing the state of French design at the exhibition that the Deco style was in the process of evolving away from its early expression, and that other foreign but related styles were at various stages of a similar evolution. Floral and geometrical motifs were equally abundant. Extravagant highly decorative palaces stood next to simple white concrete buildings, all in their different ways clamoring for attention. Bare concrete, metal and glass were the materials that best expressed absolute modernity. Mallet-Stevens had the Martel brothers design cubist trees in concrete for a garden he created on the Esplanade des Invalides – a gesture both humorous and emphatic.

A building like Mallet-Stevens' Pavillon du Tourisme was still very much an Art Deco building, despite the obvious influence of Modernism, but at first sight was utterly different in appearance from high style Deco. The slatted effect repeated over the entrance and on the tower is essentially a decorative play of planes, though it derives from Modernism and De Stijl – the stress on horizontal planes was to become an important feature of the evolved Art Deco style. This building was no less attention-seeking in its way than the department store pavilions. Proportions were exaggerated for effect, the decorative slate emphasizing the height of the tower and the low horizontality of the main building.

Many of the foreign exhibits displayed a modernity that was based on traditional types and some were barely modern at all. The Italian pavilion was a Deco revival of a classical building, though much more revival than Deco. The Japanese pavilion was traditional and picturesque in style but, rather inconsistently, it was highly praised in the official catalogue, the French being too enamored of its Oriental neatness, clean lines and functionality to admit that it was not particularly inventive or modern. The English pavilion was an extraordinary hybrid of styles. Many countries, particularly those of Eastern Europe leaned heavily on their own folk traditions for inspiration.

The Wiener Werkstätte exhibit shows that the Werkstätte style had grown away from the severe geometry of its early designs and had become rather graceful and feminine. Recurrent motifs were floral and figurative. The Czechoslovakian display was chiefly composed of simple and bold glassware – Cubism was still a dominant influence, as it had been a decade earlier. This dynamic modernistic style must have impressed the French designers. The Constructivist ceramics, graphics and paintings in the Russian pavilion were particularly

Left: The Czech pavilion, designed by Josef Gočár.

admired, as was the Swedish Orrefors glass.

For foreign exhibitors and visiting designers, the Expo was a powerful influence and stimulus. The impact it had on the work of the English ceramicist Susie Cooper, for example, was obvious and immediate. She devised a highly individual and successful style, based on and as a result of having visited the exhibition.

Despite the absence of either a Bauhaus or a De Stijl exhibit (the Dutch government refused to allow De Stijl to participate, despite Van Doesburg's pleas), Modernism was represented by Le Corbusier's controversial Esprit Nouveau pavilion and the Russian pavilion, and to a lesser extent by the Czech and Danish pavilions. Le Corbusier caused controversy with his pavilion even before it was built, and the Ministère des Beaux Arts ordered the erection of a high fence around the area for the opening of the exhibition. The pavilion was uncompromisingly stark and completely devoid of decoration, and Le Corbusier, being forbidden to cut down a tree on the site, had incorporated it extremely successfully into his design. All this drew a good deal of attention to his presence at the exhibition. Unfortunately the furnishings were less successful – he filled the interior with unmatched pieces of office furniture and cheap bentwood chairs, with a few Cubist paintings hung about the empty wall spaces.

The public might not have liked the Esprit Nouveau, but if they looked about them they would have seen plainly that the Art Deco style was following behind at a discreet distance. The exhibition marked the mid-way point in the evolution of Art Deco. It was also fundamental to the dissemination of the style both geographically, through Europe, and socially, down to a popular level. When Deco threw its doors open to the public it became popular taste.

Below: Le Corbusier's stark and controversial Esprit Nouveau pavilion was designed around a tree already on the site.

2
FURNITURE

Opposite: Emile-Jacques Ruhlmann's coiffeuse and bench in palisander, ivory and tortoiseshell (executed by Porteneuve), c. 1926, is typical of his restrained and classical style.

The story of the birth, growth and waning of Art Deco is best begun with a study of the furniture of the period, from the beginning of the century to the mid-1930s. At first glance it is difficult to see any connection between the earlier style, still firmly rooted in historicism, and the spare angular creations of the late 1920s. Yet a progression can be traced: a clear and unbroken evolution that owes its impetus to social and economic change, the example of the fine arts and architecture, and the increasing influence of Modernism. A will to simplify and be modern is the guiding principle but this is tempered with a desire to maintain comfort, chic and a sense of luxury, and a refusal to give way to anonymity and mass production.

For some years into the first decade of the century, fashionable furniture design contined to be dominated by the Art Nouveau masters, but the popularity of the style was rapidly dwindling. Art Nouveau had failed to provide a lasting modern decorative idiom, and patrons and designers began to scorn its excesses, in latter years so insensitively plagiarized for the mass market.

Although no specific style was to develop for some years, designers and craftsmen were guided by a desire to abolish the decorative hyperbole of Art Nouveau and to reassert the superiority of French design. A more rigorous style was sought, one that could keep pace with developments elsewhere in Europe (chiefly in Austria and Germany) but which was also identifiably French; maintaining, or rather reasserting, the French characteristics of luxury, refinement and high standards of craftsmanship. There was a reversion to simple, classical, elegant shapes; designers began to revive French styles of the late eighteenth and early nineteenth centuries. These borrowed styles were brought up to date with unusual combinations of materials and a stricter application of ornament. Focus shifted to the elegant forms of the furniture and decoration became confined mainly to flat surfaces, enhancing the lines and planes of a piece.

All manner of embellishments for those flat surfaces were devised, and in all kinds of exotic and rare materials. Rich veneers became fashionable, often applied to a cheaper and more robust structure. Warm woods were prefered, or woods with distinctive grain patterns such as amboyna, walnut, palmwood, zebrawood, Brazilian jacaranda and the dark striped macassar ebony. Ebony was a particular favorite, always highly buffed to a deep glossy finish. Many of the woods used were extremely rare, brought from southeast Asia or Africa. Sometimes tooled *repoussé* leather was applied as a surface embellishment, or fine leathers and animal skins such as morocco, vellum, snakeskin or tortoiseshell (sliced very fine to near transparency).

After a lapse of nearly 200 years shagreen was revived as a decorative material. This was the hard scaly skin of a breed of dogfish, which was bleached and sometimes tinted. It was applied in small sections and its patterned texture greatly appealed to Art Deco designers. A fine ivory inlay was used as a complement to

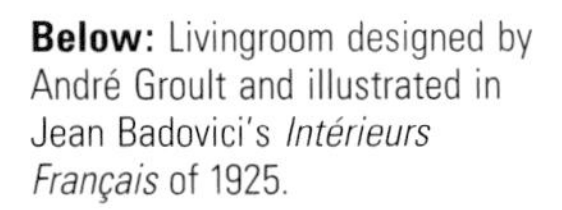

Below: Livingroom designed by André Groult and illustrated in Jean Badovici's *Intérieurs Français* of 1925.

Left: This commode in silvered wood with incised decoration and silk tasseled handles was designed by the Atelier Martine; neat and geometrical in form with opulent touches.

shagreen or dark wood veneers; drawer pulls were carved from ivory and furniture legs were tipped in ivory. Sometimes a number of materials, silver, mother-of-pearl or ivory, were combined in a marquetry design.

Oriental lacquer, made from the sap of a tree and applied to wood or a metal ground to create a hard, bright, smooth surface, was immensely popular in the 1920s. Lacquering is a laborious process but can be used to achieve a wide range of decorative effects. Pigments or minerals can be used to color the lacquer, gold and silver leaf can be embedded in it, and it can also be carved or encrusted with ivory, mother-of-pearl or hardstones.

Despite the emphasis placed on high quality cabinetry and craftsmanship, designers tended not to be craftsmen themselves. Very few of the top designers had more than a rudimentary technical knowledge. The large companies had their own cabinetmakers, while independent designers had their pieces made up by artisans working in the Saint-Antoine district of Paris.

Surviving records of private, commercial and government commissions show that Art Deco was a widespread taste, but the most significant source of patronage came from the fashion world. Led by Jacques Doucet and Paul Poiret, the top Parisian couturiers (most of whom were women – Jeanne Lanvin, Suzanne Talbot, Madeleine Vionnet) became the great promoters of the new style; they had their homes and their salerooms decorated with modish extravagance by their favorite designers and the results were much publicized. Initially the elaborate, high Deco style predominated, sponsored by wealthy patrons many of whom had recently joined the ranks of the rich and who sought a style that was both modern and comfortably within the bounds of tradition.

Paul Iribe is recognized by many as being the most important early exponent of Art Deco. He began his career as a caricaturist and his work was spotted by Poiret, who commissioned him to design an album of fashion plates. His talent was confirmed and Poiret set him designing furniture, fabrics, jewelry and rugs. In 1912 he was commissioned to decorate Doucet's apartment in the Avenue du Bois. Iribe's career as a furniture designer was short-lived, however, and by 1915 he had abandoned it for Hollywood and a new life creating film sets for Cecil B de Mille and others. Iribe's abilities as a

Right: Armchair by Paul Iribe, a major early exponent of Art Deco design whose work continued to show traces of Art Nouveau linearity.

Below: Armchair in macassar ebony, *repoussé* leather and ivory, c. 1925, designed by Clément Mère, another designer influenced by Art Nouveau.

draftsman are apparent in his calligraphic handling of design, which gives his work an insubstantial, brittle quality. He was one of the few Deco designers whose furniture continued to display the linear quality more associated with Art Nouveau – in his case a linearity that was always disciplined by an *ancien régime* elegance.

In the case of Clément Mère, it was his fondness for large areas of surface decoration that betrayed the lingering influence of Art Nouveau. As the Art Deco style matured, decoration became more controled in its application and Mère began to be criticized for over-embellishing his pieces. He started his career as a painter and worked his way from fine arts to applied arts, at first designing exquisite toiletry items and then graduating to furniture design in around 1910. This sort of career progression was typical of many Deco designers.

The basic structure of Mère's furniture was derived from eighteenth-century models but it was often almost completely covered in floral decoration, most characteristically in tooled *repoussé* leather. These floral designs were rather vague, loose and meandering, again reminiscent of Art Nouveau. There was also an element of Eastern exoticism in the richness of his textures, colors and decorative effects.

Another designer belonging to this early group was Clément Rousseau. He specialized in rich juxtapositions of fine materials, often in bold geometrical patterns, applied to simple structures that were based on late-eighteenth-century prototypes. His preference was for rich grained woods like palmwood or rosewood, which he set with stained shagreen (often in contrasting tints) or snakeskin. He was one of the first to revive the use of shagreen and to combine it with an inlay of fine bands of ivory.

Süe et Mare represent the fully fledged floral manner of high Art Deco. They were one of the first companies to offer a complete decorating service and helped to establish *ensemble* and *ensemblier* as keywords during this period. Spurred on by the example of the Deutsche Werkbund and Wiener Werkstätte, French furniture designers became increasingly concerned with the harmonizing of a room's décor. This did not mean a literal application of motifs from one piece to another, but rather a more imaginative general coherence of style, requiring a sense of proportion, pattern and color.

André Mare was a painter turned decorative artist. From around 1910 he was increasingly drawn to furniture and interior design, and in 1912 exhibited his 'Cubist House'. This was considered at the time to be terribly avant-garde but in retrospect was emphatically not; a little decorative angularizing on the facade was the only (very remote) reference to Cubism,

Above: This pair of chairs in rosewood, inlaid with sharkskin, ivory and mother-of-pearl, c. 1925, by Clément Rousseau, shows his juxtaposition of rich materials and simple classical shapes.

Left: Dressing-table and stool in burled ash and aluminium, 1933, by Süe et Mare, who found themselves obliged to keep pace with changes in design but were never really at home with the modernistic style.

Right: Side-chair in ebony and stained tortoiseshell, designed by André Groult and painted by Marie Laurencin, c. 1924.

which was never very apparent in the work of the traditionalists. The interior was in the pompous, bourgeois style that was to become characteristic of Mare's work with Süe. Louis Süe was trained as an architect, but he too became involved with interior decoration around 1910 and worked briefly for Paul Poiret. Süe and Mare met just before the outbreak of the war and began to work together when it was over. In 1919 they set up their Compagnie des Arts Français, more usually referred to as Süe et Mare, a partnership that lasted until 1928. They undertook architectural and decorative commissions and employed a prodigious team of collaborators who worked on schemes for embassies, shops, nightclubs and the luxury oceanliners. Companies likes theirs were forming in response to an increasingly competitive market and a general trend toward consolidating design services.

Süe et Mare's furniture was traditionally inspired, mostly by the Empire style but also partly based on provincial designs. A very superficially Cubist treatment is also evident. Carved tassels, *bombé* legs, formalized drape effects and curving contours are typical of their *oeuvre*: very much traditional forms gently brought up to date. They were also masters of the floral cluster, which was partly based on rococo motifs and partly derived from the conventionalized blossoms of Oriental art. Their company produced a complete range of objects and furnishings including fabrics, wallpapers and rugs; smaller items such as clocks and mirrors often also sported floral clusters.

There is nothing aggressively modern about Süe et Mare's work, and they said themselves that they did not aim to be avant-garde but simply to create pleasant and comfortable surroundings for their customers. Their interiors were indeed comfortable, colorful and warm, with densely patterned walls and floors. In 1921 they published what might be called a manifesto, *Architectures*, in which they justified their adherence to past styles. They represented those designers who reacted against Modernism and who stood resolutely for comfort and a sense of luxury and repose in an interior, which they said was needed more than ever before in the modern age, with all its stresses.

When Art Deco matured into its modernistic phase, Süe et Mare made a rather grudging attempt to adapt their style – in the march towards Modernism they brought up the rear. Despite their attempts to keep pace with fashion, they suffered financial difficulties in the late 1920s, and in 1928 their company was taken over. Nowadays Süe et Mare pieces are much sought after and fetch fantastic prices, rivaled only by works by Ruhlmann.

Also working in the traditionalist vein was Jules Leleu, whose simple forms, overlaid with a veneer of warm woods, were unremarkable and often derivative but for a characteristic scattering of tiny leaves and flowers inlaid in ivory and mother-of-pearl. This flowery signature made his work unusually fresh and charming. He was one of the few designers to execute his own designs, and his cabinetry was always of the highest quality.

André Groult began to exhibit at the Salons around 1910. His work was simple and his forms comfortable and solid; most of his pieces were designed to co-ordinate with the soft muted colors of paintings or wallpapers by Marie Laurencin. His most famous *ensemble* was the lady's bedroom in the French Embassy at the 1925 Exposition, with its curved forms clad in pale shagreen and its *bombé* chest of drawers in shagreen trimmed with ivory (the shagreen paneled to emphasize the swollen contours) – an extraordinary piece, with a faint, erotic suggestion of the female form.

Emile-Jacques Ruhlmann was in many ways the brightest star in the Art Deco firmament. His admiration for the *ébénistes* (cabinetmakers) of the late eighteenth century inspired him to strive for the highest standard of design and workmanship, and he can fairly be said to have attained those ideals in his work. He had an unfailing sense of elegance, proportion and harmony and a willingness to pare forms down to their minimum, displaying far greater restraint than any other designer working in the traditionalist manner. His furniture was highly exclusive, affordable only by a few.

Ruhlmann's first furniture designs were exhibited at the Salon d'Automne in 1913. He had no formal training in cabinetry, but made drawings which were scaled up and then passed on to a cabinetmaker. In 1919 Ruhlmann founded a company with Pierre Laurent. Slowly they built up their clientele and their workforce. His designs continued to be inspired by neoclassical furniture, and decoration was always minimal: just a hairline of ivory inlay sketching a pattern of diagonals, or a row of little ivory dots accenting form and line, a charming and brilliant device for softening the severity of his designs. In some cases silk tassels or ivory rings used as drawer pulls provided the only ornament. He employed Dunand to lacquer and Georges Bastard and Mme O' Kin Simmen to execute the ivory carvings and inlays he applied to his pieces. He used expensive warm woods such as amaranth, amboyna and ebony as veneers, while desks and dressing tables were inlaid with fine leathers such as morocco, snakeskin or vellum. In the late 1920s he developed a more minimalist and streamlined style making use of materials such as chromium-plated metal, silver and glass; his forms became squatter and more geometrical and lost their neoclassical references.

Left: Carved macassar ebony cabinet inlaid with silver and mother-of-pearl by Süe et Mare, 1927.

Below: Emile-Jacques Ruhlmann's *Grand Salon* from his Hôtel du Collectionneur at the 1925 Exposition; the painting over the fireplace is by Jean Dupas.

Ruhlmann was also a master *ensemblier*. He set his furniture in environments that were less hectically patterned and vibrantly colorful than those of most of his contemporaries, and achieved a sense of comfort and discreet opulence. He designed carpets, fabrics and wallpaper as well as tableware and lighting fixtures. His schemes were characteristically monumental, with lofty ceilings, gigantic cascading chandeliers and over-scaled wallpaper patterns. He drew around him the best of the Deco designers; the list of those who collaborated with him at the 1925 Exposition is impressive: Brandt, Decoeur, Décorchemont, Dunand, Jourdain, Legrain, Lenoble, Linossier and Puiforcat are the most notable. It was the Exposition that truly launched him and made his work known. His Hôtel du Collectioneur (home of a patron of the arts) was lauded by critics and public alike, and he became the focus of French pride in the reinstatement of its traditional supremacy in furniture design. Throughout his career Ruhlmann argued the importance of good craftsmanship and art for the elite. He was very far from being a Modernist, yet he contributed to the evolution of the Art Deco style by making pure, virtually undecorated forms fashionable.

Printemps was the first of the four great Parisian department stores to establish a design studio, Primavera, opened in 1912, and to market up-to-date furnishings by artists of repute at reasonable prices. The other stores followed suit in the early 1920s: Galeries Lafayettes with La Maîtrise, Le Louvre with Studium-Louvre and Au Bon Marché with Pomone. Recognizing that the growing and increasingly affluent middle class was becoming more discriminating, they replaced those manufacturers who had been foisting their outmoded designs on a dissatisfied public and met the demand for good design that was both relatively inexpensive and also fashionable and thoroughly modern in feeling. This was an important step on the road to making good design available to all classes through mass production.

Right: Cheval mirror in burled amboyna with fine ivory inlay, designed by Emile-Jacques Ruhlmann and showing his minimal use of decoration.

Below: Corner cabinet in lacquered rosewood inlaid with ivory and rare woods, 1916, by Emile-Jacques Ruhlmann.

The department stores offered a complete range of furniture and household goods, providing an interpretation of Art Deco that was neither extreme nor expensive. By popularizing the style they also helped to define it.

Maurice Dufrène was long associated with La Maîtrise studio, taking over its artistic direction in 1921. He was energetic and extremely versatile; he made an easy transition from Art Nouveau and later, with equal facility, adopted the modernistic style when it became fashionable. As long as the quality of goods was maintained, Dufrène was always in favor of using industrial methods of production to help cut costs. His style was unremarkable, a clever synthesis of the dominant trends in design.

The Pomone studio was run by Paul Follot from 1923. He was a staunch traditionalist and absolutely opposed to the mass production of art, but could not prevent Pomone from adopting the modernistic Deco style when he left. His taste for rather florid carving and elaborate surface decoration was no doubt carried over from his early association with Art Nouveau.

The high Art Deco style based on traditional forms did not have many important exponents abroad. In Britain there were a few half-hearted attempts to imitate the French style. At the Paris Exposition Sir Edward Maufe exhibited a desk in mahogany, camphor and ebony, gilded with white gold; its materials and tasseled draw pulls were inspired by French design, but it was altogether too heavy and inelegant to bear proper comparison. In general the British furniture industry was paralyzed by the lack of any creative opportunities and continued to turn out period reproductions of distinctly varied quality.

A few designers in Germany were working in the Parisian mode. They catered for a bourgeois elite, and based their designs on German

Left: Table in lacquered wood patterned with crushed eggshell, c. 1925, designed by Jean Dunand, a sculptor who turned first to metalwork then to lacquer.

Below: Armand-Albert Rateau's bedroom for Jeanne Lanvin's home, 1920-22, one of his best known commissions.

Above: Jean Dunand's four-paneled screen in silver and black lacquer, c. 1928, shows his mastery of lacquerwork.

Below: Eileen Gray's furniture designed for Suzanne Talbot, c. 1920, is more abstract in style than her opulent early work.

baroque. Like the Parisian designers, they sought rich veneer and inlay effects but the results were undistinguished, lacking the grace of the French style.

Not every French designer who sought a new style around the second decade of the century looked back to French tradition for inspiration. Alongside the work of the traditionalists, which was fashionable up to the mid-1920s, there was a tendency among certain designers to explore the art forms of other cultures – notably of the Far East and the Middle East – in a move to break with past styles and create a truly modern idiom. The Cubists launched a fashion for tribal African art, which Doucet helped to absorb into the decorative arts and which stimulated in its turn a borrowing from other primitive and early art forms. Cubism itself was an important influence, encouraging designers to explore the decorative possibilities of geometric abstraction and the fragmentation of form.

These sources of inspiration had a very liberating effect on Art Deco, stimulating some highly original work which showed how far interpretations could diverge and yet still be part of the same style. In general the increasing urge toward simple forms and sparse decoration was more pronounced in the work of those artists exposed to non-French cultural influences, which reflected a more durable aspect of Deco, bridging the gap between the traditionalist and the modernistic styles.

Paul Poiret set the example in borrowing from foreign themes and created a style that influenced both the traditionalists and those who sought a less 'historical' decorative idiom. He founded his Atelier Martine in 1911; by encouraging very young girls to draw and paint

Above: Eugène Printz's bedroom ensemble in palmwood, exhibited at the 1926 Salon of the Société des Artistes Décorateurs.

from nature, he established a source of spontaneous and colorful design. His style incorporated these designs and at the same time owed a great deal to the Ballet Russes and the flamboyant exoticism they had made popular. He launched a fashion for opulent interiors, with a rich confusion of pattern, color and texture on floors, walls and upholstery. Low divans and day beds were heaped with multicolored silk-tasseled cushions and pillows. Furniture was neat and geometrical, clearly influenced by Weiner Werkstätte design.

Armand-Albert Rateau was an unusual designer who developed a style based on Egyptian, Persian, Syrian and Antique art; walls, doors and screens were covered with delicate, stylized, silhouetted flora and fauna, with a few exquisite pieces of furniture in patinated bronze, oak and lacquer taking up the same motifs. He sculpted animals, charming, attenuated and graceful creatures which he arranged as supports to chairs, chaises longues, tables and standard lamps. From 1920 to 1922 he decorated Jeanne Lanvin's apartment on the rue Barbet-de-Jouy. The walls of the bedroom were hung with a blue silk fabric that was embroidered in white and gold thread in the Lanvin workshops. His famous low bronze table supported by four birds also stood in the bedroom. The bathroom was equally luxurious, with an abstract pattern of marble inlay on the floor and a low relief stucco panel set into one wall depicting birds, deer and fronds. The fittings were in marble and bronze, and animal skins were strewn over the floor and furniture.

A sculptor who turned to metalwork and then to lacquer, Jean Dunand was one of the most versatile of the Deco designers. He learned the lacquer technique in 1909; tradition has it that he traded the secrets of his hammering technique for those of lacquerwork with the Japanese lacquer master Sougawara. He began by using lacquer to embellish his metal vases but became enamored of the technique and gave up metalwork to concentrate on the design of lacquered furniture, chiefly cabinets, panels and screens. The *laque arraché* method, which involved roughening and then gilding the top surface of the lacquer in order to achieve a gradation of tones, became a particular speciality of his. Dunand also revived the use of eggshell in lacquerwork and created a variety of different effects by sealing pieces of eggshell into a lacquer ground.

He established a system of collaboration with a number of designers, lacquering pieces for Printz, Ruhlmann, Legrain and others. He also executed decorative designs by Schmied, Jean Lambert-Rucki and Paul Jouve. Dunand's furniture was generally of the simplest design

with all the decorative interest confined to the lacquered surfaces. Early compositions tended to be strong abstract geometrical designs, while later on he began to diversify in response to the demands of a larger clientele, and added stylized animal subjects and *japonisant* or African figures to his repertoire.

Many of the most avant-garde and innovative designers of Art Deco were protégés of Jacques Doucet. He was an inspirational patron and influenced the development of a more modernist idiom. The designers he commissioned to decorate his home were encouraged to create interiors that would complement his collection of avant-garde art and Negro sculpture. The furniture was by Eileen Gray, Marcel Coard, Pierre Legrain and Rose Adler.

The work of Pierre Legrain was particularly marked by his long association with Doucet. He was discovered by Iribe and collaborated on the Doucet decorating commission of 1912 as Iribe's assistant. It was certainly due to his association with Doucet that he came to be interested in Cubism and African tribal art, which had a profound influence on his furniture design. This is evident in the fierce

geometry of his work; a prelude to the modernistic Art Deco style. A number of his pieces were directly derived from African tribal furniture. His work was simple and monumental, with a focus on form and smooth surfaces, accented with color and minimal abstract ornament.

Eileen Gray was born in Ireland and settled in Paris in 1902. She trained as a lacquerer in

Above: Interior of Le Corbusier's Esprit Nouveau pavilion at the 1925 Exposition; the paintings are by Le Corbusier and Fernand Léger.

Opposite above: Le Corbusier, Jeanneret and Perriand's *ensemble* with three chairs in tubular steel, c. 1929; this type of innovative interior design was a significant influence on modernistic Art Deco.

Left: Bed in palisander, silvered metal, ivory and bakelite, c. 1930, designed by Marcel Coard in modernistic Deco style.

Opposite below: Pierre Legrain's black lacquered chaise longue incrusted with mother-of-pearl and upholstered with zebra skin, c. 1925, is typical of his simple geometrical style.

London and then in Paris under Sougawara. Her early furniture designs date from around 1910 and all the pieces were lacquered. This early work shows the influence of Oriental and African forms and motifs, yet is extraordinarily modernistic for the time. Colors are subdued and decoration minimal; all the novelty of design is concentrated on form and the enhancement of form. Doucet spotted her work at the Salon des Artistes Décorateurs of 1913 and the following year commissioned some furniture from her. The lacquered table she designed for him, with leg capitals carved in the shape of lotus blossoms, stems in ivory and dark-green lacquer, hung with huge silk tassels and rings of amber, is characteristic of her sophisticated and opulent early work. After the war she designed interiors for the milliner Suzanne Talbot (Madame Mathieu-Lévy), her first commission as an *ensemblier*. The rooms were dramatically bare but for the flying arabesque motifs that decorated carpets and walls and furniture was minimal. By this time she had abandoned figurative designs altogether in favor of abstraction.

In the mid-1920s she began to avoid the luxurious materials and the refinement and theatricality of her early style to concentrate on designing functional, compact, multi-purpose pieces intended to inhabit Modernist spaces.

At about the time that Marcel Breuer and Ludwig Mies van der Rohe were introducing tubular steel into their designs, she was doing the same. This change of direction corresponded to her growing fascination with modern architecture and Modernist theories. Her later work is truly Modernist in intent and cannot be considered as Art Deco.

After 1925, when the first experiments with tubular steel furniture were being made and the theories of the Modernists were becoming familiar and even appealing, Art Deco began to adapt to the new design currents. The new interiors were created partly in response to the change in building styles; apartments were smaller, lighter and more practical and required furnishings that were both compact and functional.

Many of the changes that came about in the decorative arts were due to the influence of the Bauhaus, which emphasized the use of new materials, the improvement of cheap manufacture and the creation of models appropriate for series production. The function of an object was the prime dictator of its design and so ornament became redundant. The Bauhaus artists were among the first to create tubular steel furniture, and much of this furniture, such as Marcel Breuer's cantilever chair, is so simple and archetypal that it has remained in production ever since. The influence of De Stijl, with its emphasis on the build-up of planes, also became absorbed into Modernism, particularly through the work of the architect and designer Gerrit Rietveld.

Le Corbusier played a fundamental role in the dissemination of Modernist theories, and helped to publicize and further the innovations of the Bauhaus. In collaboration with the designer Charlotte Perriand he created three chairs in tubular metal, all important prototypes in the history of design. Eileen Gray's Modernist work includes pieces that were multi-purpose and movable, made from tubular and perforated metal, glass and celluloid. She developed almost a mania for designing furniture that would pivot, swivel, fold away or slide to and fro on runners. Her Transat armchair is a famous piece, based on a deckchair design, with a padded seat slung on a lacquered and chromed frame.

The bentwood chairs that Thonet had patented in the nineteenth century were acknowledged as an important influence on these designers; Le Corbusier, for instance, filled his Esprit Nouveau pavilion at the 1925 exhibition with them. A number of designers recognized, virtually simultaneously, that simple lightweight structures in tubular steel similar to Thonet's bentwood frames would be easy to mass produce and could represent an attractive and versatile point of departure for a new design aesthetic. One of the great advantages of metal was that it withstood the drying effect of central heating which was so damaging to woods. The rise of Modernism had much to do with the introduction of metal furniture. Initially many people put up a great resistance to metal, condemning it as too clinical and characterless. Le Corbusier's tubular chairs, particularly his chaise-longue, perplexed and enraged the public. The group of Art Deco designers who took up metal tubing and demonstrated how it could be made chic and luxurious by the addition of rich materials – lacquer, leathers, marble and smoked glass – did much towards making it acceptable. Inevitably machine-age simplicity and materials did become fashionable, and metal furniture gradually became standard in home and office.

Above: Pivoting nest of tables, c. 1924, by Pierre Chareau, who designed solid angular furniture to complement Modernist architecture.

Opposite above: René Herbst's diningroom, c. 1930, epitomizes the new stripped style.

Opposite below: Armchair, c. 1920, by Pierre Chareau.

The urge to pare down forms and abbreviate ornament that was always a tendency in Art Deco, became quite exaggerated under the influence of Modernism. Yet Art Deco retained most of its characteristics, its interest in elegance and refinement and its mannered quality. Furniture became simpler, more geometrical, compact and unadorned, with an emphasis on planes. The harmonized *ensemble* was still important but, in place of the cluttered effect of pattern on pattern, came a play of light and space and an arrangement of a few well chosen pieces.

From the early 1920s, a group of designers that included Francis Jourdain, Pierre Chareau, Robert Mallet-Stevens and René Herbst argued against the elaborate high style in favor of a stripped style that was absolutely modern and practical rather than primarily decorative. Some leaned more toward Modernist theories than others, but they all promoted an aesthetic that was modernistic; a stylish and distinctive version of Modernism. In their wake followed a group of less ardent modernistic designers, who compromised with strict Modernism and allowed the style to lapse back a little into a more comfortable and luxurious mode.

The Union des Artistes Modernes was established in 1930, its five founding members being Hélène Henri, René Herbst, Francis Jourdain, Robert Mallet-Stevens and Raymond Templier. Together they consolidated the attitude to design they had each pursued individually in their work, and at the 1930 Salon des Artistes Décorateurs they made a stand by exhibiting separately. Even by the next year their role had become redundant, since what they strove for had largely been achieved.

Although most Art Deco designers did not concern themselves with the problems of mass production and the democratization of design, the influence of Modernism, the new minimalism and the use of cheap, easy-to-manufacture metal furniture began to make modern design a general taste. Firms were established offering cheap furniture in metal or laminated wood; bright, simple and well-designed.

The architect Pierre Chareau designed furniture and interiors that complemented the new architecture; not furniture that rose on tapering legs, but solid, comfortable, sculptural forms, with an angularity derived from Cubism, which set off architectural features and enhanced the spatial setting. He had a fondness for contrasting curving lines with straight and overlapping pivoting planes, which allowed a table or desk to be enlarged or contracted and added subtlety and interest to the rigid geometry of Modernism. He also had a taste for unusual materials, although he did design furniture with traditional rich veneers and colorful patterned upholstery. He explored the use of glass and mirror; flat iron banding, which he used as a framework for some of his furniture; alabaster shades, for his lighting fixtures; studded rubber flooring, which he used throughout

Below: Pair of armchairs and small table covered in shagreen, c. 1927, designed by Jean-Michel Frank, who combined an austere line with expensive materials.

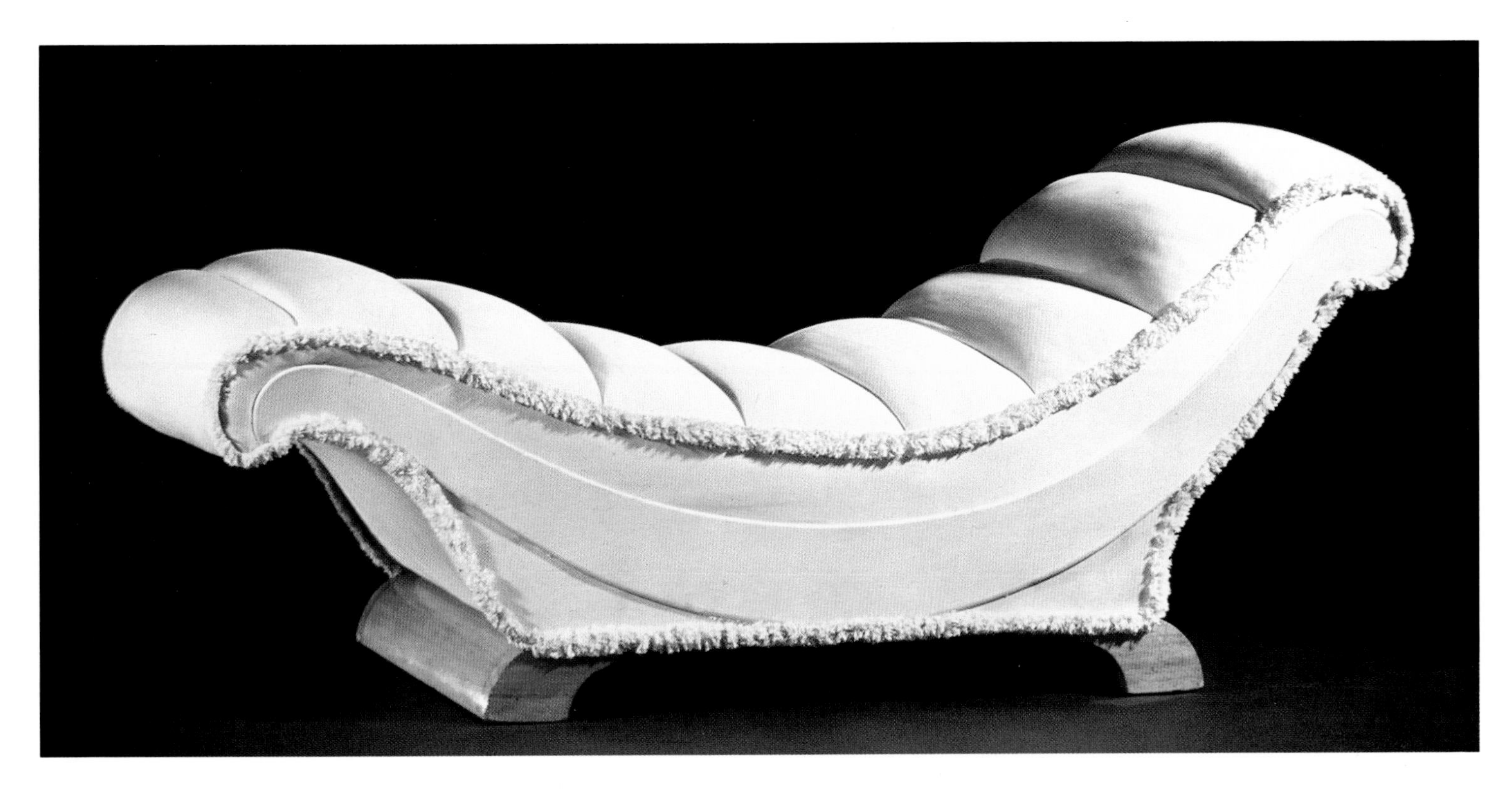

his Maison de Verre (constructed from 1928 to 1932); and he pioneered the use of plastic as a practical surface in children's rooms and bathrooms. The social implications and aims of the Modern Movement did not, however, concern Chareau. He worked throughout his career for a rich and discerning elite.

René Herbst designed uncompromisingly stark furniture from the start of his career in 1919, and denounced as outmoded the high Deco style. His best designs date from the mid-1920s when he was working a great deal in tubular steel. Shop fronts and window displays were his speciality. His designs were always very rigorous and logical, with a subtle elegance and careful balancing of proportions. Decorative details were few but distinctive and focused particularly on lighting fixtures; a

Above: Betty Joel's chaise longue in beechwood, upholstered in cream silk, c. 1930, bears comparison with the work of Frank.

Below: Sideboard and chair, c. 1930, by the Modernist architect Alvar Aalto.

Right: Ludwig Mies van der Rohe's cantilever chair in tubular steel, c. 1929; Mies van der Rohe was the first to exploit the flexibility of tubular steel.

lamp hovering like a butterfly over a dining table, or a standard lamp composed of a metal disk sitting at a jaunty angle atop a tubular metal support.

Robert Mallet-Stevens is more famous as an architect, but he did design furniture and interiors too and began exhibiting as a decorator around 1913. His furniture and interior design, like his buildings, are very angular and crisp, with a stress on horizontal planes that is almost decorative. Much of his furniture incorporates a slatted effect which is relieved or broken up by checkered or irregular geometrical patterning on carpets, curtains, upholstery, floor tiles and even light panels. This geometrical treatment was characteristic of the work of many modernistic Deco designers, and was related to the streamlining effect adopted from American Deco. Mallet-Stevens painted his tubular furniture in bright colors and used Hélène Henri's fabrics for upholstery.

As early as the first decade of the century Francis Jourdain was preaching the need to unfurnish space and keep ornament to a minimum, letting the function of an object determine its design; his only concession to luxury was an occasional rich veneer. Later on he actively promoted the design and production of inexpensive furniture. His pieces were simple, geometrical and solid-looking, designed with the requirements of the smaller modern apartments in mind.

There were other designers who adopted the modernistic Deco style mid-career and promoted an expensive mannered version for a fashionable and rich clientele. Eugène Printz changed his style around the time of the Paris Exposition, having previously worked in an *ancien régime* idiom. An elegant interplay of curves and straight lines characterized his work, which was easy, refined and luxurious. Printz designed metal furniture as well as continuing to use expensive woods and developed a distinctive and innovative style.

Left: Denham MacLaren's table in glass, wood and chromium-plated metal, 1931, is typical of his idiosyncratic style.

Jean-Michel Frank designed in a very austere modernistic style but used expensive materials to create rich textured effects and a feeling of luxury. He covered walls and furniture in suede and parchment and upholstered in velvets, silks and suedes. His interiors were colored in natural tones and lighting was muted and concealed. He made straw marquetry his specialization, a laborious technique that required individual lengths of straw to be split and glued.

The new design current affected all designers, who were obliged to adapt in order to remain competitive. The result was that companies such as Süe et Mare made concessions to the new fashions and turned out superficially modernistic pieces that incorporated the new materials, especially metals and glass.

The high Deco style bypassed Britain, and by the late 1920s, when it was organized to compete with France and Germany, Modernism was the trend. Because this was not a style based on specific historical precedent, it was easily assimilated and British designers were soon contributing their own strong Modernist style.

Below: Betty Joel's kidney-shaped desk, c. 1930.

Serge Chermayeff introduced the first tubular metal furniture to Britain, which he marketed through the furniture store Waring and Gillow. He, Jack Pritchard and Wells Coates spent some time visiting the Bauhaus and absorbing ideas, and later set about applying the same approach to design in Britain. The company PEL (Practical Equipment Limited) was set up in 1931 and produced ultra-modern smart furniture along tubular lines. Tubular steel very quickly became popular and inspired all sorts of innovative designs. At the same time a good deal of cheap mass-produced furniture began to flood the market – insensitive renderings of modernistic themes, with indiscriminate use of geometric motifs and lots of sharp angles.

Betty Joel set up a company with her husband in 1919 and produced simple functional pieces that were also sophisticated, in a style that was closest to the luxurious Modernism of Printz or Frank. Many of her commissions were for decorative schemes for hotels, shops and offices. She also produced inexpensive easy-care furniture for the modern working woman and influenced the cheaper end of the market, which copied many of her designs. The designer and decorator Syrie Maugham helped to promote a glamorous Hollywood-style modernistic Deco that became popular in the 1930s; a fashion for mirror, glass and chromium plating everywhere, deep carpets in abstract designs and minimalist furniture. She was particularly known for her all-white schemes. Mirrored and glass furniture became all the rage, and lent a dramatically glittering note to sober interiors, amplifying the sense of space and light. Mirror was particularly associated with the ubiquitous cocktail cabinet.

A remarkable furniture designer of this period was Denham MacLaren although he remained relatively obscure, partly because of his small output. Using all the standard materials of modernistic Deco, including glass and plated tubing, he invented highly unusual and sophisticated pieces.

In Finland the Modernist architect Alvar Aalto initiated serial production furniture and in 1931 established a firm in Helsinki, Artek, which manufactured furniture, lighting fixtures and fabrics in a Bauhaus style adapted to traditional materials and designs.

Elsewhere in Scandinavia, particularly in Sweden, a strong style emerged in the late 1920s, influenced by Bauhaus functionalism. Lightweight, practical, simple shapes were set in airy Modernist spaces. Bruno Mathsson was the best known of the Swedish designers and his very successful line of bent and laminated wood furniture was designed with comfort as well as function in mind. The architect Erik Gunnar Asplund developed a style that blended Modernist with classicist tendencies.

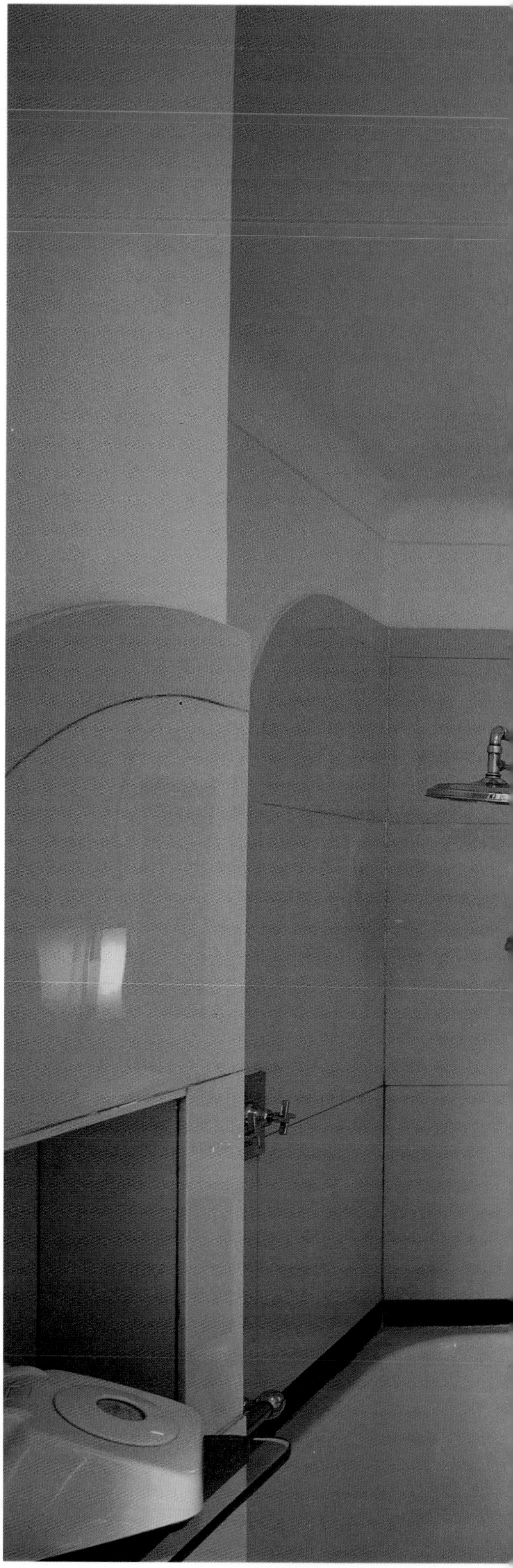

Opposite: Bathroom of Claridges Hotel, fitted in modernistic Deco style, London, 1930s.

3
TEXTILES

Opposite: *'La Danse'* block-printed repeating fabric design, c. 1910, by Raoul Dufy, who drew on eighteenth-century examples in his work.

Until the Art Deco period textile manufacturers were still running through the deadly repertoire of period designs. General developments in the decorative arts and the changing aspect of the modern interior, however, divorced textiles from conventional designs and conventional attitudes to the role they should play in an interior. This was a discipline in which women were particularly prominent.

Paul Poiret, who played such an important role in the development of a modern French style in furniture and interior decoration was equally involved in liberating textiles from their dependency on past styles. The girls in his Atelier Martine produced bright, colorful, naive designs based on observations of nature, the best of which were transposed onto fabrics, wallpapers and carpets. Poiret conceived of a new style of decorating in which simple geometrical furniture was set against walls and floors that were covered in these vibrant designs. Inspired by the décors created by Léon Bakst and others for the Ballets Russes, he jumbled patterns, colors and luxuriant satiny fabrics for a rich exotic flavor. Although the fashion for this elaborate decorative chaos was short-lived, the effect of warm and lively textile designs juxtaposed with relatively plain pieces of furniture, was one sought by the majority of Art Deco decorators.

In most interiors of the high Art Deco period (up to the mid-1920s), walls and floors were covered with complex patterns that repeated the standard repertoire of Deco motifs and provided a rich surface covering as well as a unifying element in a room. A liking for the Atelier Martine pattern-on-pattern effect lingered on, with inlay and marquetry designs on furniture set against patterned carpets and wallpapers.

It was clear at the 1925 Exposition that the textile industry was lagging behind the other decorative arts in the quest for modernity, and was too reliant on traditional designs, and too pictorial. Eventually, as furniture became plainer, the role of textiles grew increasingly important. In overall patterned environments the clean forms of exquisite pieces of furniture were set off to advantage. Ruhlmann always used pattern to contrast with simple pieces of furniture and to unify an *ensemble*.

In the context of Modernism and Le Corbusier's insistence that walls should be white and unadorned, textiles became one of the few decorative accents (or even the only one) in otherwise rather austere interiors, and designers came to see the role of textiles as providing the main source of warmth, color and pattern in a

Below left: *'Les Cactus'* wallpaper design by Atelier Martine.

Below right: Louis Marcoussis's carpet, c. 1926, was bought by Jacques Doucet for his studio at Neuilly.

Left: Tapestry, c. 1927, by Gunta Stadler-Stölzl, whose Bauhaus workshop was extremely influential in its radical approach.

room. They also began to make use of new synthetic materials together with new methods of production.

Walls became plainer, carpets shrank in size, patterns were less hectic and obtrusive, and color schemes were either subtle and muted or based on a single primary color. At the Bauhaus Gunta Stadler-Stölzl ran an important weaving workshop and encouraged experimentation with weaving techniques and use of new materials. The Bauhaus workshop exercised a massive influence in its liberation of color, its abolition of conventional decoration and the generally fresh approach it took to tex-

Above: Marie Laurencin's tufted wool carpet, 1934, is reminiscent of her paintings (page 161).

tile design. In France too there was a move towards using synthetic fibres and exploiting varying techniques of production, in order to create textural effects and abstract patterns.

In common with the other disciplines of the decorative arts, textile design drew inspiration from a range of sources including Cubism, primitive arts, Oriental and Middle Eastern art. There was a basic progression from dense florid designs to abstract geometrical ones.

Most of the great *ensembliers* involved themselves in the design of textiles: Maurice Dufrène, Emile-Jacques Ruhlmann, Süe et Mare, Eileen Gray, Paul Follot and Francis Jourdain, to name a few of the best known. They recognized that textiles were not a casual addition to an *ensemble* but needed to be carefully integrated. Eileen Gray, for example, clearly took as much care in the design and placing of her rugs as she did with any piece of furniture.

Carpets and fabrics of the Art Deco period have not survived well to the present. Textiles are by nature ephemeral – they fade and wear out, making it difficult to give an exact assessment of the output of any period. Fortunately numerous photographs and colored albums of designs help to fill this gap.

CARPETS

In the high Deco phase carpets were large (often wall-to-wall), highly decorative and colorful. Designs were generally floral and fruity, in the French tradition; Dufrène, Groult, Follot, Ruhlmann and Süe et Mare all designed knotted carpets patterned with flowers. Marie Laurencin was an exception in this group, for she applied themes recurrent in her paintings – young girls and animals in soft pastel colors – to the carpets she designed. Several carpet manufacturers, perceiving that the developments in design were becoming popular, commissioned work from well-known Deco artists such as Follot, Süe et Mare and Robert Bonfils.

Ivan da Silva Bruhns was the greatest of the French rug designers of the period, and the designer who first applied a modern approach to the medium. As was true of all artists who revolutionized design in their different fields, he took a great interest in craftsmanship and materials, and even developed a variant of the traditional knotted stitch. He was equally concerned with the function of a carpet in an *ensemble* and developed his style in keeping with the tendency to simplify and geometricize. He marketed his own designs and provided carpets for a number of *ensembliers*. His early carpets incorporate motifs such as the key pattern borrowed from Greek art. He was also strongly influenced by Berber designs and techniques of rugmaking which he would have known from the exhibitions of Moroccan art held in Paris from around 1915. He worked in deep, rich, earthy tones, reminiscent of the natural dye colors of Berber rugs. In later years his designs became more abstract, incorporating a Cubist application of overlapping geometrical shapes which he often interspersed with rows of dots or notches.

When Doucet was furnishing his Neuilly studio he commissioned carpet designs from the painter Louis Marcoussis and adapted cartoons by the sculptor Gustav Miklos. They both worked in a dramatic Cubist-inspired style setting a precedent in Modernist carpet design.

Eileen Gray also pioneered a simple abstract style of carpet design which she sold with the furniture from her shop, Jean Désert. These were small rugs with deep luxurious piles and bold abstract designs. Some were quite loosely woven and textured to contrast with glossy lacquered surfaces. Carpets in her *ensembles* always had a very precise function. In the interior she designed for Suzanne Talbot she repeated on the carpets the motifs that decorated the walls, so that the furniture seemed to float in an environment of swirling shapes. Elsewhere rugs were designed and placed to draw together the different elements in a room, and as such played a role both focal and dramatic.

In Modernist interiors carpets became important additions to the setting, providing color, warmth and a note of individuality in the midst of all the near-identical tubular furniture. As if the carpet had risen in status and was now asserting its importance in the general scheme of a room, designs grew large, bold and also sculptural, with patterns cut into the pile in relief, and an emphasis on texture. At the same time carpets shrank in size, and furniture was arranged around and over it to create interesting sculptural juxtapositions. Carpets were frequently used to accent architectural features or emphasize spatial play; Chareau, for example, placed a round carpet by Jean Lurçat beneath the cupola of his study-library in the Ambassade Française at the 1925 Exposition.

A number of good carpet designs came out of England during this period, most of them designed by women. Betty Joel used Da Silva Bruhn's rugs in her interiors for a time, then began to design her own. These were simple and understated, often in creamy tones.

The graphic designer Edward McKnight Kauffer and his wife Marion Dorn were both successful designers of avant-garde hand-knotted carpets, though Dorn was the more brilliant. She made carpet design her specialization and developed a technique of cutting the pile to create interesting textural patterns. Kauffer's rugs were decorated with bold geometrical patterns and were often used by the decorators Raymond McGrath and David Pleydell-Bouverie in their interiors.

WALLPAPER AND FABRICS

The high Deco style in wallpaper, as typified by Süe et Mare's *ensembles*, was a lush all-over covering of flowers and fruit within a geometrical framework, a grid or a trellis. Emphasis was on color combinations. André Groult was influential in commissioning designs for block-printed cloth from other artists for use in his interiors. Ruhlmann applied bold, over-scaled, repeating designs to his walls and upholstery. Many *ensembliers* designed large ranges of different textiles and printed papers to complement their interiors, and the Parisian department stores produced various light Deco and, later, modernistic designs to go with their furniture. Pictorial compositions of contemporary *fête champêtres* designed by André

Above: Hand-knotted wool carpet, c. 1930-33, by Ivan da Silva Bruhns, most innovative of the French designers.

Below: Axminster rug, c. 1925, designed by Edward McKnight Kauffer.

Left: Tapestry wall-hanging, 1921, by Marianne Geyer-Pankok; in Eastern Europe, traditional folk art was blended with Deco influences.

Left: *Simultané* shantung fabric, 1926-27; by Sonia Delaunay in her characteristically geometrical style.

Mare, André Marty and Charles Martin were frequently printed up as room hangings or made into screens.

Not surprisingly, tapestry upholstery was popular with the traditionalist designers and enjoyed a revival during this period. The French had an enduring reputation as great tapestry masters, but standards had rather fallen in the nineteenth century, with a wealth of second-rate pictorial designs dominating output. By the 1920s most of the large decorating firms and department stores were marketing screens and seat furniture upholstered in tapestry. A number of tapestry manufacturers of long standing, such as Aubusson, La Manufacture Nationale de Tapis et Couverts de Beauvais and La Manufacture Nationalė de Gobelins, retained their own design team. Jean Lurçat worked for Aubusson in the 1930s and succeeded in singlehandedly reviving the art of tapestry by applying geometrical designs and creating compositions that focused on the interplay of colors or on textural contrasts. Chareau used Lurçat's tapestry designs to upholster his furniture. But the old habit of reproducing contemporary paintings in tapestry

Below: Süe et Mare's gilt wood and tapestry salon suite, the tapestry executed from a design representing the story of *Paul et Virginie* by Charles Dufresne. The suite was exhibited at the 1925 Exposition.

lived on; in the late 1920s and 1930s Marie Cuttoli, who worked for Aubusson, commissioned major artists such as Matisse, Picasso and Léger to design tapestry cartoons. On the whole, however, the results were too painterly and therefore inappropriate to the medium, and did not achieve great success.

One of Poiret's protégés, Raoul Dufy, was an inspired fabric designer as well as a painter and graphic artist. His designs were influenced by the narrative eighteenth-century style, with small but elaborate repeating scenes of fishermen, tennis-players and dancers. He also designed the standard decorative fruit and floral fabrics and papers. From 1912 to 1928 he worked for the Bianchini-Férier textile company. He exhibited wall hangings in Poiret's barges at the 1925 Exposition featuring fashionable ladies in fashionable locations: at the races, the casino, a regatta. The example Dufy set by involving himself with textile design encouraged many young designers to contribute to the revival of the industry and the craft.

Below: Fabric by Hélène Henri woven with geometrical motifs.

Sonia Delaunay was another of the leading fabric designers of the period. She worked in a dynamic geometrical style, creating abstract patterns in mainly primary colors which were based on a variant of Cubism called Simultaneism which she and her husband had developed. In the years before World War I she became interested in fabric design through experiments with color relationships and juxtapositions. Her work was much imitated and began a fashion for contrasting color schemes. Her dress fabrics were always conceived with a view to the appearance of the pattern when worn and the way they might complement the movement of the wearer.

The Modernists, led by Le Corbusier, declared war on wallpaper. In the late 1920s the taste for bright color schemes waned and in its place came a fashion for subdued, earthy, neutral tones which lasted through the early years of the Depression. This shift in emphasis was accompanied by the abandonment of printed fabrics and a concentration on the textures of woven fabric. In France Hélène Henri, founder member of the UAM (Union des Artistes Modernes), set up a craft-weaving workshop in the early 1920s and became the chief exponent of this new style, which owed much to the influence of the Bauhaus. The raw material was exalted and new synthetic fibres incorporated; rayon and cellulose among others. There was no need for printed decoration. Good weaving, it was felt, was beautiful in itself; varieties of weaves were explored and unusual materials such as straw were woven into the fabric for interesting textural effects. Heavy upholstery materials such as tweed contrasted well with metal frames. Hélène Henri's fabrics became very fashionable and were used by Mallet-Stevens, Jourdain and Chareau among others. Her designs were based on thick weave plaids and stripes, or repeating geometrical motifs in neutral tones. Designers like Jean-Michel Frank covered walls in plain textured fabrics, vellum or suede.

The Omega group take much credit for revolutionizing printed fabrics in England, and introducing abstract and geometrical designs, although the effect on the textile industry was delayed until long after the war. Just as British furniture design remained largely unaffected by the developments in France, so too did textile design languish until the late 1920s.

William Foxton, owner of a textile company, was one of the few who fed good designs by talented artists into the textile industry. In the 1920s he sought out designers capable of creating an exciting modern idiom for fabric design. The stark silhouetted angularity of Vorticism translated particularly well as a decorative style, and many dynamic and interesting abstract patterns were produced.

Another important contribution to English textile design was made by the Phyllis Baron and Dorothy Larcher partnership. They concentrated on block-printed fabrics, both updated floral chintz-types and bold geometrical designs. They specialized in the Indian method of bleaching a pattern onto a colored ground, known as discharge printing. Later on they were joined by Enid Marx, a talented artist who designed an extremely successful range of upholstery fabric for the London Passenger Transport Board. Marion Dorn was better known for her sculpted carpets but she also produced some simple inexpensive fabric designs for the old Bleach Linen Co. Ltd for which she, with Paul Nash, was principal designer.

In around 1910 the Wiener Werkstätte had established a separate textile division to provide carpets and fabrics for specific interiors. The results were so successful that the workshop was enlarged and an independent retail outlet established in 1917. Early textiles designed by Koloman Moser and Josef Hoffmann were austere – rigidly geometrical with monochrome checks and herringbone patterns. From the late 1910s, however, bright color and lively decorative motifs began to creep into their designs. Dagobert Peche was one of the most brilliant of the later designers, working in a style that was based on Austrian baroque and rococo motifs.

A group of designers in Germany produced designs more akin to Deco than to the Bauhaus work. Marie Hannich, for instance, applied angular geometrical renderings of images of ships, cars and buildings to fabrics. Textile design in Denmark, Belgium and Scandinavia was modernized along similar lines. Traditional forms of weaving were combined with folk or primitive designs that were angularized and applied alongside geometrical ornament. In Russia bright textiles and wallpapers incorporating abstract geometrical designs – some rather alarmingly exuberant – were designed by avant-garde artists such as Varvara Stefanova and Liubov Popova, as part of the general attempt to create a totally new idiom.

Above: Printed linen, 1922, by Gregory Brown for William Foxton.

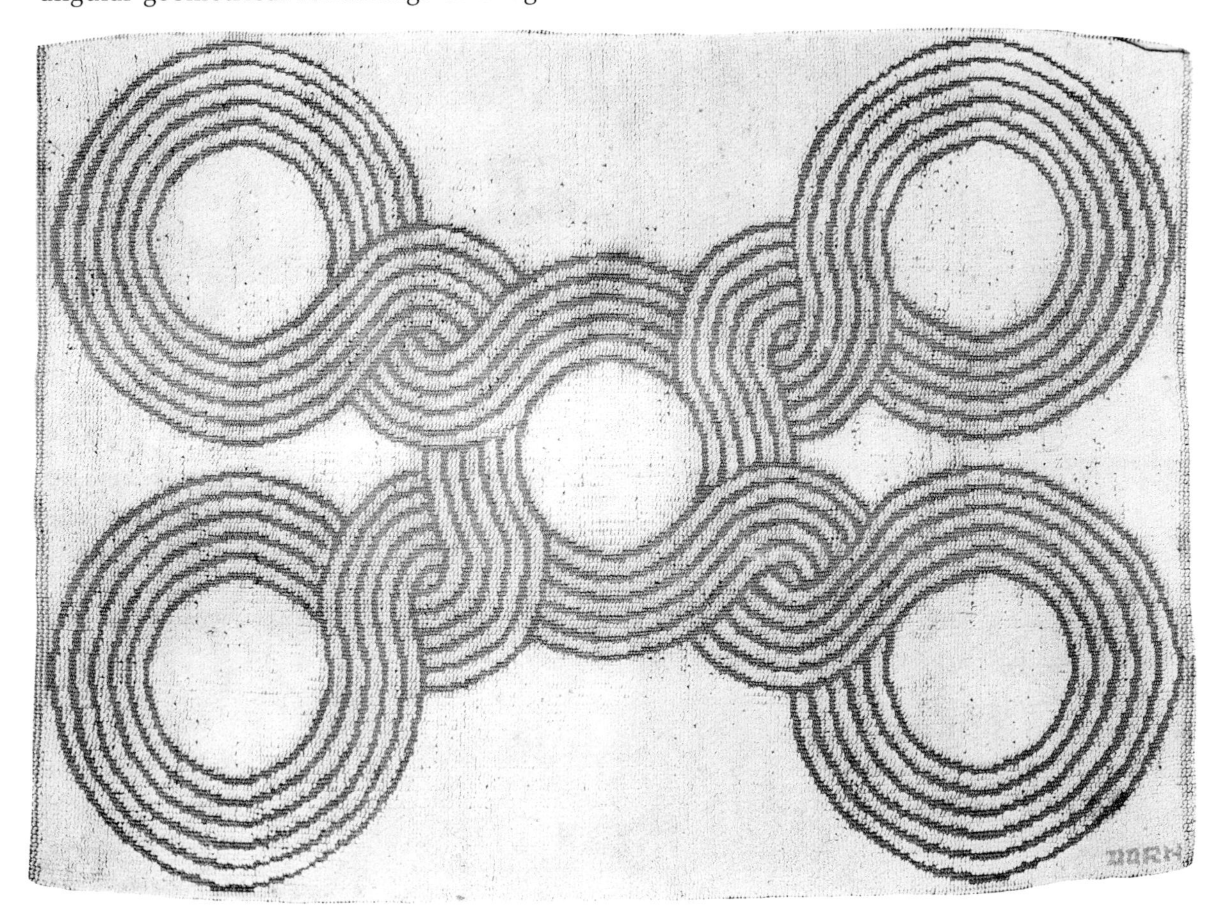

Left: Woven carpet, c. 1935, by Marion Dorn.

LIV 1928
JEAN GOULDEN

4
METALWORK

Opposite: Silvered-bronze and enamel clock, 1929, by Jean Goulden, one of the chief exponents of Deco enamelwork.

Metalwork of the Art Deco period was particularly strongly dominated by Parisian design. The output of the period is not easy to characterize, yet this much can be said of all the best work, from the magnificent wrought-iron creations of Brandt to the simple hammered metal pots of Linossier: that there is a consistency of approach, a sensitivity to the metal, and an exploitation of its properties for decorative ends.

During the nineteenth century French ironwork had given up trying to compete with the obvious economic advantages of foundry work and had gradually gone into decline. The great Art Nouveau designers Guimard and Majorelle had certainly contributed to the renaissance of the craft of the *ferronier*, but at the turn of the century the industry was still enfeebled and iron was cast into the most insensitive historical plagiarisms. By the 1920s the craft was fully revived and modernized, and beginning to win back the reputation it had earned for itself in the eighteenth century.

Its great versatility made ironwork suitable for adaptation to modern design; it could be made to appear massive and crude or delicate and refined. Various patinas could be applied to its surface and iron could be combined with other metals such as brass, copper, steel and aluminum. Recent scientific advances in the field of metallurgy had shown that there was enormous potential for varying treatments and methods of production. As long as the designer was skilful and imaginative, there were endless design possibilities. Once ironwork had regained its popularity a wide variety of objects

Right: Girault shopfront, Paris, c. 1925 (Azema, Edrei and Hardy, architects); an example of the ornate ironwork that was applied to façades in the early Deco period.

became available, from jewelry and small objects to monumental architectural features.

The new atmosphere of daring and innovation in design encouraged decorators and ironworkers to rethink the role of iron and other metals in an interior. A single piece of ironwork as a focus to a room was always successful; it added an element of precision and monumentality. Console tables topped by a richly grained slab of marble were popular, as were screens, chandeliers, mirror frames and firedogs in iron. With the advent of modern conveniences in homes and offices, ironwork acquired new roles. The ugly radiators that were a necessary adjunct of central heating installations could be disguised with ironwork screens, which neither disturbed the air flow nor were damaged by the heat. In new apartment and office blocks ironwork lift cages were installed, often highly decorative and designed to match balustrades and entrance doors. Ironwork was also imaginatively applied to the exteriors of buildings: balconies, grilles, and particularly shop-fronts. Decorative screens backed in glass became very popular as shop doors, and designs were often extended to frame windows and incorporate lettering cut or cast in iron, presenting a unified and distinctive façade. As modern buildings became more austere, ironwork was often the only element of decorative relief on a façade.

The high Art Deco style with its stylized motifs – sunbursts, fountains, doves, gazelles and endless floral fantasies – adapted well to ironwork. When the style matured and these motifs were replaced by more rigorous abstract

Left: Entrance doors of the Maison Paul Poiret on the Champs Elysées in Paris, with metalwork by Edgar Brandt, c. 1925.

Right: Albert Cheuret's 'Egyptian' clock in silvered bronze and onyx, c. 1930.

forms, ironwork was versatile enough to adapt but other metals more suitable to the expression of that style also came into their own.

Much of the credit for the highly successful revival of wrought-iron goes to Edgar Brandt, undisputedly the leading exponent of the period. His technical mastery of the material and his exploitation of the various properties of the metals he worked with, earned him this unrivaled reputation. In the interest of achieving new decorative effects, he varied color, tone and patina and in later years experimented with combinations of metals, using new alloys such as 'Studal' and steel as well as aluminum to create striking contrasts. He developed techniques which allowed him to present a highly finished appearance and to disguise the methods of construction. He also perfected a virtually invisible seaming technique known as autogenous welding that gave his work a particularly smooth finish. He often worked in close association with other designers and artisans, and was always prepared to execute other people's designs. Brandt was not a craftsman who jealously protected and promoted hand-crafted work and he used industrial techniques whenever it was possible to do so, in order to cut corners without jeopardizing the quality of the finished product. He used stamping presses, for instance, to repeat patterns.

Below: Süe et Mare's gilt-bronze clock, c. 1924, is in their typically floral style.

Brandt's work was essentially in the high Art Deco tradition, incorporating most of the characteristic motifs of that period in a characteristically mannered and refined style. He worked the iron into deceptively fluid, delicate and graceful forms based on scrolls and flowers. His many public commissions for buildings and monuments, as well as collaborative projects with architects and interior designers and private commissions for homes and hotels, required him to design and execute shelving systems, room dividers, radiator covers, fire screens, lamps, stair rails and balconies.

In the early 1920s Brandt opened a showroom in Paris where he exhibited glassware, ceramics, jewelry and other crafts which complemented his designs, alongside his own ware. One of his most successful pieces was the serpent standard lamp with alabaster or glass shade, called 'La Tentation'. From as early as 1910, Brandt formed an association with the Daum glassworks. They provided glass shades, often acid-etched or smooth and opaque, for his wrought-iron supports and fixtures.

As for many of the best Art Deco designers, the Paris Exposition was the making of Brandt's career. He exhibited widely, but his most significant contributions were the Porte d'Honneur – the main entrance to the exhibition – and the five-paneled 'Oasis' screen. His gift for successfully applying decoration to a monumental work was clearly demonstrated in the massive gateway, which he designed in collaboration with André Ventre and Henri Favier. A grille of repeating fountain motifs linked groups of columns topped by more stylized fountains. The project was also a measure of Brandt's technical skill, for it was an achievement in itself to succeed in endowing the cheap alloy 'staff' with the qualities of a more noble metal. Brandt also provided objects and furniture for Ruhlmann's pavilion at the exhibition, and furnished his own pavilion in ironwork throughout. The Oasis screen was the *pièce de résistance*; it is more angular in style than Brandt's early work, and large chevron-patterned leaves are a striking element of the design. A streamlined fountain flows against a background of these large variegated leaves in iron and brass. After the Exposition, Brandt became a designer of international repute. By 1926 he had established overseas showrooms in New York and London.

Like Brandt, Raymond Subes was apprenticed to the great Art Nouveau ironsmith Emile Robert and, like Brandt, he was extremely prolific. Subes' technique was much simpler, however, and was popular because he achieved rich and elegant decorative effects at relatively low cost. He also explored new techniques and in particular methods of industrial production which he applied to his designs for both furniture and monumental architectural pieces. Whenever he could do so without sacrificing the quality of hand-crafted pieces, he used machines to ease his work, mainly for cutting and polishing. Subes contributed to the general advance toward Modernist ideals by striving to maintain artistic quality as well as to make pieces easy and cheap to produce, and by incorporating industrial techniques which for too long had been anathema to designers. His style evolved alongside the general development of Art Deco; in the early 1920s he was working in a very delicate scrolled style, while

Above: Wrought-iron fire screen, early 1920s, by Edgar Brandt, master of Deco metalwork.

Below: Raymond Subes's console table in wrought-iron and marble, c. 1925, is typical of his simpler more delicate style.

Right: Edgar Brandt's interior panel of a lift cage for the new entrance loggia of Selfridges department store, London. The panel was adapted from a design of 1922 entitled *Les Cigognes d'Alsace*.

his exhibits at the 1925 Exposition show that he was moving towards a decorative idiom that was more angular and less elaborate. He finally evolved the fully Modernist mode, developing an exceptionally strong geometrical style. Like Brandt he worked mostly in wrought-iron, which he occasionally combined with bronze or copper and, in later years, with steel and aluminum.

Various other wrought-iron masters deserve

mention. Paul Kiss was a Romanian who settled in France and collaborated for a while with Brandt and his work displays a similarly lyrical quality. He worked in a distinctive style that combined angular forms with floral and scrolled motifs. His work was distinguished by its *martelé* decoration, a treatment that involved hammering deep incisions into the metal.

The Nics *frères* company was formed by two Hungarian-born brothers who had settled in Paris. They designed and crafted a wide range of decorative ironwork, mostly architectural but also some furniture. They gave their work a hammered finish, and developed a simple angular style.

Bronze was Rateau's metal; its archaic-looking greenish patina complemented his designs, and the skill required to work it made it an expensive luxury, in keeping with the refinement and exclusivity of Rateau's interiors. Bronze was previously the preserve of locksmiths, and Rateau was responsible for reviving its use in furniture.

Fontaine et Cie were a Parisian firm who were bold enough to take on all kinds of commissions in the decorative hardware line from fashionable Deco designers. Süe et Mare used them a great deal to execute designs for clocks, mirrors and light fixtures in their characteristic floral style. Maurice Dufrène also had a taste for ironwork and used Fontaine et Cie for his designs, including a dining room in wrought-iron

Above: Edgar Brandt's *Oasis* five-paneled screen in wrought-iron and gilt-bronze, made in collaboration with Henri Favier and featured as one of the prime exhibits at the 1925 Exposition.

Left: Raymond Subes's stainless steel grill, set with cabochons of Lalique glass.

Right: Lacquered vase decorated with crushed eggshell, 1923-24, by Jean Dunand.

Far right: Hammered and chased nickel-silver vase inlaid with silver, 1926, by Claudius Linossier.

and glass, the table supported by a clever system of curved metal ribbons.

As the streamlined modernistic look took over from high Art Deco, new alloys began to replace the more traditional metals. These were lighter and cheaper to produce without being any less strong. Highly polished tubular metals were used architecturally, most typically in the form of railings which accentuated the horizontal lines of a building and were often the only decorative element on a façade.

Below: Enameled copper vase, c. 1925, by Camille Fauré.

The development of steel tubing allowed furniture designers to create a new idiom; light frames, smooth surfaces and neat forms. Much of this tubing was chromium or nickel plated, with a glossy reflective finish that distinguishes Deco furniture from the severe functionalist designs of the Modernists.

The abundant ironwork flourishes on shopfronts were replaced by neater, starker, but no less distinctive designs in metal and glass. Mallet-Stevens clad the façade of the Bally shoe shop in riveted plates of brass. Other shop fronts were totally plain except for the lettering that ran across the façade in a three-dimensional design cut from sheet metal.

In Britain, the fancy high Parisian style of metalwork was adopted, but it was cheaply reproduced and was generally used to decorate cinemas and hotels.

DINANDERIE AND ENAMEL

Dinanderie is the name given to the art of hand working objects from non-precious metals, usually by hammering. A single sheet of metal, usually copper, lead or pewter, is teased into a vase, platter or bowl form with infinite skill and patience. The metal has to be constantly reheated to make it soft and malleable, and a variety of tools has to be used, working inside and out, to shape the metal and control its spread. The revival of dinanderie work owed much to the great surge of interest in Japanese art.

What is characteristic of the work of the artists who specialized in dinanderie is their sensitivity to the materials and their skill as craftsmen. Although many of their pieces were decorated, it was the tone and surface treatment of the metals that assumed prime importance, and articles were lovingly fashioned, with all the potential for contrast between shadow and reflected light fully exploited.

The decoration of these objects is equally painstaking work. Patinas are achieved by applying acids, metal oxides and a naked flame. Sometimes the surface is carved or chased, or else is inlaid with other metals. This involves grooving out a design, then filling it with a plug of softer metal and hammering it into place. A pleasing effect is achieved if the two metals are then heated so that they fuse into one another slightly and the tones mingle and become smoky.

Jean Dunand was the grand master of dinanderie. He grew up in Geneva, and in 1896 won a scholarship and came to Paris to study sculpture. He became apprenticed to the sculptor Jean Dampt, who was an admirer of the English Arts and Crafts movement. Under Dampt's influence he began gradually to abandon sculpture and became a metalworker, handcrafting his pieces in the most arduous fashion. In the early years of the century he was exhibiting works in a late Art Nouveau style, rather overblown and not at all true to his real taste, which eventually led him to create plainer forms. He abandoned these bulbous organic shapes and after 1918 concentrated on abstract patterns which he applied to enhance forms. His best work is very simple and elegant, a marriage of Oriental, African and traditional influences; round gourd-shaped or elongated vases, the surfaces worked with patinas, chiseling and overlays in gold and silver and decorated with abstract incrustations. He worked in a variety of metals including lead, nickel and steel. In his later work he abandoned decoration altogether and concentrated on creating pure forms, absolutely plain except for a very striking lacquered finish in brilliant color, mostly blacks, reds and golds.

Once he had mastered the technique of lacquering Dunand began to apply lacquer to his hammered metal forms. He fully exploited the technique of *coquille d'oeuf* (the application of fragments of eggshell) for its decorative potential. With all the possible gradations in tone and texture, in combination with gold and silver leaf and different colored lacquers that this technique offered, Dunand was kept busy devising a seemingly limitless repertoire of decorative treatments for his dinanderie. He became so absorbed with lacquerwork that he gave up metalwork to concentrate on creating largescale lacquer designs and also lacquered furniture.

Left: Jean Dunand's hammered copper vase, gilded and patinated, early 1920s.

Below: English silver and enamel cigarette case, c. 1931.

Right: Lift shaft in the Grunfeld department store in Berlin (Otto Firle, architect).

The other important master of dinanderie of this period was Claudius Linossier, who worked chiefly in copper. His work is subtle and understated, its abstract ornament derived from ancient art forms, the metal inlays expanded and fused into one another to create smoky, shimmering tones. Linossier's admiration for Etruscan pottery led him to experiment with metal incrustation, which became his speciality. He was also concerned with enriching surface texture, by creating special alloys with unusual tonal effects or by burnishing the metals, though he rarely tried to disguise the rough unpatinated surface of copper.

Maurice Daurat worked exclusively in pewter, experimenting with form and with treatments that would enhance the soft, ductile, heavy quality of the metal. His forms were pure with an absolute minimum of decoration.

Elsewhere in Europe the German firm Württembergische Metallwarenfabrik, who were most famous for their Jugendstil objects, adapted the Parisian Art Deco style in the 1920s and produced a successful range of metalwork objects in a light, rather stereotyped decorative style, not nearly as sensitive as the work of the French metalworkers. At the Bauhaus in the 1920s, Wilhelm Wagenfeld was designing metal objects in a rather futuristic style. Marianne Brandt was the greatest German metalworker of the period, however; she joined the Bauhaus in 1924 and became renowned for her

Left: Lettering on a shopfront by René Herbst.

metal lamps. Like the silversmith Jean Puiforcat, she adhered to geometrical principles in her work.

Jean Goulden and Camille Fauré were the chief exponents of enamelwork in the Art Deco period. Goulden became fascinated by Byzantine enamelwork while staying in a Greek monastery on Mount Athos on his way home from foreign service during World War I. When he returned to France he learned the champlevé enameling technique from Jean Dunand. He worked in silver, gilded copper and bronze and his designs were rigorously geometrical, displaying the influence of Cubism. He created clocks, lampstands, candlesticks and other objects in bronze and enamel: sculptural, asymetrical compositions made up of irregular, overlapping geometrical forms. He also made boxes with compositions of triangles, circles and zigzags, sometimes with sections applied in relief.

Enamel is made by combining powdered glass with chemical pigments and fusing it to a metal base. Limoges was traditionally famous for its enamels and Camille Fauré set up his workshop in Limoges. Working on a copper ground he created colorful enamel vases, decorated with geometrical motifs, thickly sculpted in relief and in pastel color combinations. His early work was more richly colored and floral.

Below: The Citroën showroom in Amsterdam, c. 1930 (Jan Wils, architect). The runged balustrade is used to add emphasis to the horizontal lines of the building, and to provide a decorative flourish in a relatively austere interior.

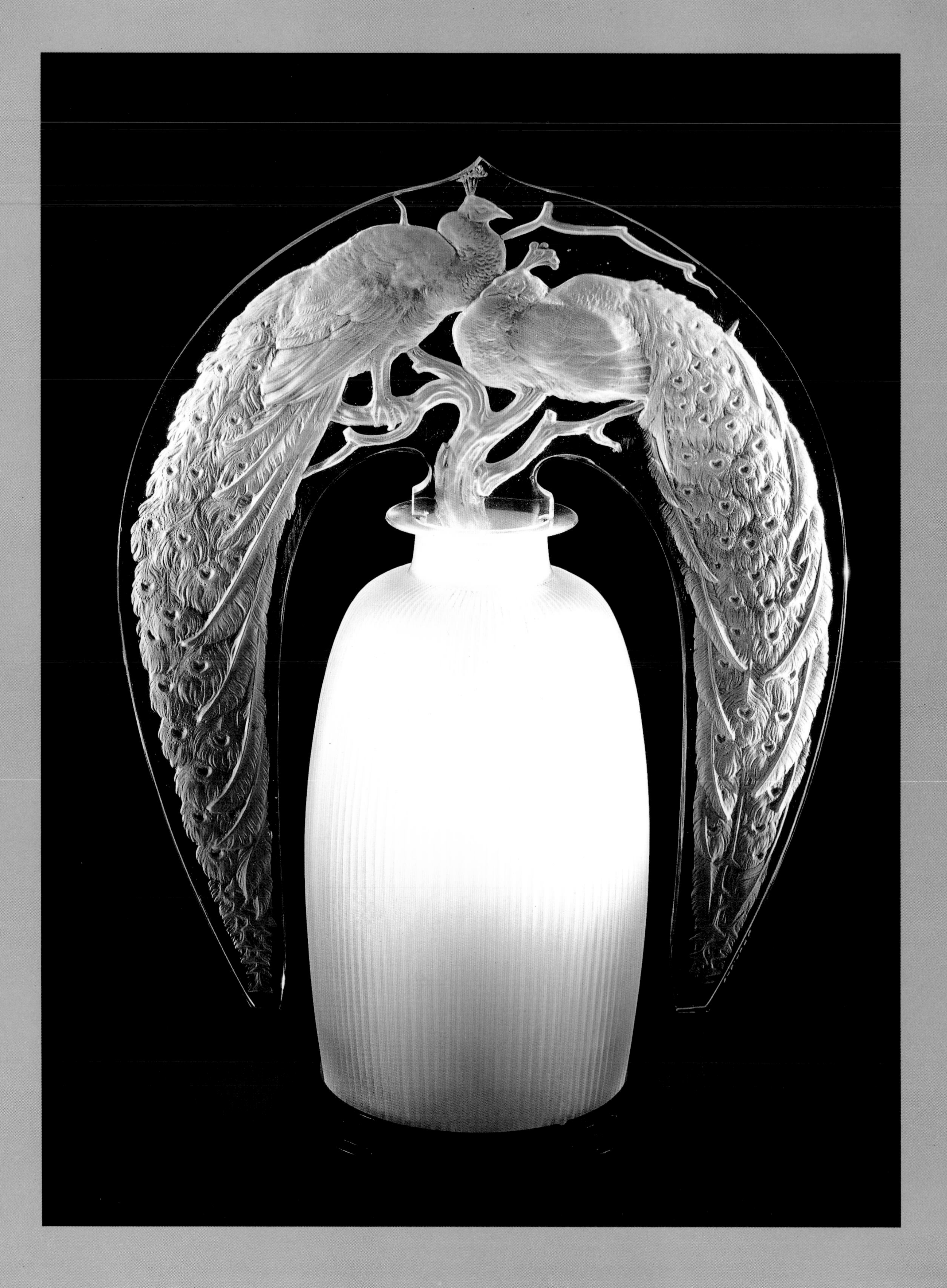

5
LIGHTING

Opposite: René Lalique's *Grande Veilleuse* table lamp etched with a peacock design.

There was a steady increase through the 1920s and 1930s in the number of people who had electricity in their homes. Electric light first came into use in the last years of the nineteenth century. By the Art Deco period it was no longer a recent invention, but it was some time before it was reliable and cheap enough to become ubiquitous, and even by the mid-1930s electricity was by no means a feature of every home. Once the system had been perfected the advantages of electric light were enormous, for it was brighter, cleaner, less hazardous, more versatile in its applications and far easier to use.

Yet it took some time before electricity was fully exploited for its lighting capacity, and designs for lighting fixtures displayed a search for maximum efficiency. Lamps were either designed in imitation of the old gas and candle fixtures or else were decorative, highly colored creations, sometimes fashioned into animal shapes and emitting only a very soft filtered glow. Designers were more concerned with magic lantern effects than with lighting rooms and banishing the gloom of centuries. In either case the tendency was to disguise the electric fittings as far as possible.

When designers finally moved away from the attractions of colored light, they began to realize the true potential of electric lighting. The gradual assimilation of electricity into daily life coincided with the period of intense creative activity in the decorative arts during the interwar period. Thus *ensembliers*, metal and glassworkers, and artists from other fields of design were drawn to explore the decorative as well as the practical applications of electric lighting, and to assign it an important role in the modern interior. Lighting became a serious concern, and competitions and Salons of Light were held frequently through the 1920s and 1930s to stimulate new ideas in design.

Below: Wrought-iron chandelier with alabaster shades, by Edgar Brandt.

Great care was always taken to eliminate any aggressive glare and to break up ugly points of light. Translucent materials such as parchment, alabaster and sand-blasted or thickly molded glass were found to filter a milky diffused quality of light that was not harsh on the eyes. The revolution in lighting began with experiments; shallow basins of thick glass or alabaster were suspended by a system of cords or chains from the ceiling to replace the redundant multi-armed candelabra form and the imitation candles. The idea of lighting from a central hanging fixture and from wall brackets remained dominant for some time.

Although the functional nature of lighting was becoming more important, lamps and light fixtures continued to be regarded as highly decorative *objets d'art*, and few designers could resist their potential for decorative effect. In an interior, the light source was frequently the most unusual and in some ways the dominant feature. This went on being true even of the most modernistic interiors of the late 1920s and early 1930s.

The marriage of wrought-iron and glass in designs for light fixtures was a highly successful one, and continued to be popular through to the mid-1920s, when it was superseded by plainer, less unwieldy designs. The weight and strength of iron contrasted well with the fragility of glass. Designs were very decorative, in the scrolled and floral manner favored by the wrought-iron masters. Lamps of glass blown into a wrought-iron armature and often made up into animal shapes were a particular fashion of the period. Their effect when lit was of pure light trapped in an iron mesh.

Edgar Brandt was producing iron *torchères* and wall sconces from early on in his career and around 1910 he formed an association with the glass manufacturers Daum. His rearing serpent standard lamp, complete with early Daum shade in a marble effect of swirling color, was extremely popular and was sold in three sizes. Later on, when Daum was concentrating on heavier glassware etched with floral or geometrical designs in grainy and smooth textures, the style was still strong enough to complement Brandt's designs; and often the decorative motifs of the armature were repeated in the acid-etched design of the shade. Brandt did not exclusively use Daum glass, and on occasion worked with Lalique and other manufacturers, but his work was particularly well suited to Daum's glass designs.

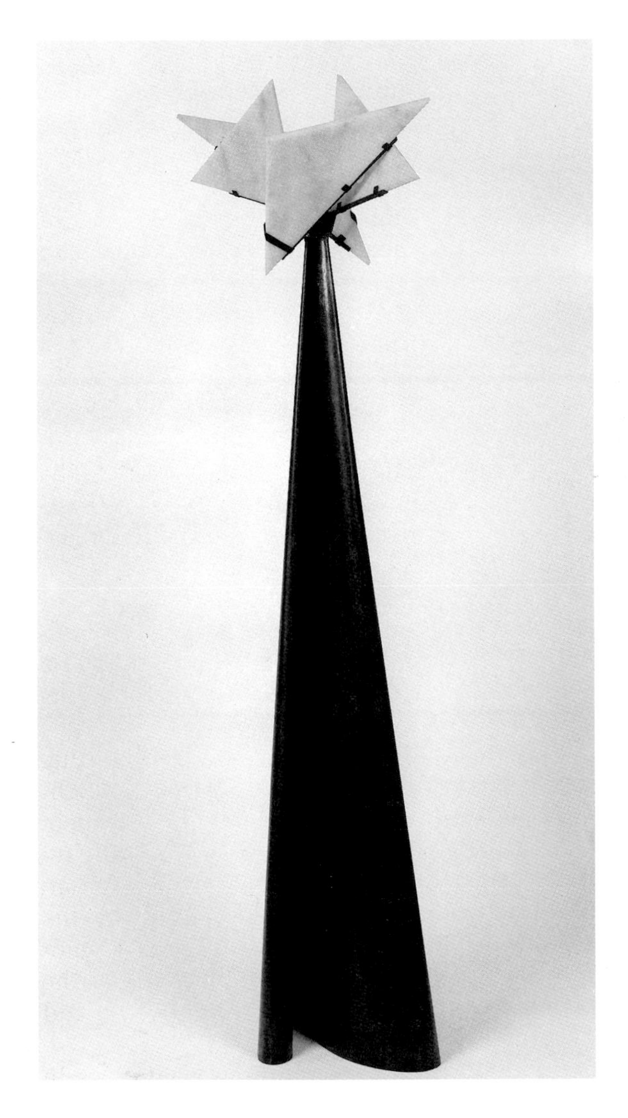

Above left: Pierre Chareau's Cubist-inspired *La Religieuse* lamp, with metal standard and shade made up of sections of alabaster, 1923.

Above: Edgar Brandt's wrought iron chandelier, with etched glass shades by Daum, c. 1925. Brandt worked in association with the glass manufacturers Daum from about 1910.

In addition to producing glass shades for the wrought-iron masters, the Daum firm also manufactured an innovative range of glass lamps of their own design. Many of these were cast in mushroom or cylindrical shapes; the glass was thick, generally in white and creamy tints, and acid-etched with strong geometrical designs. Sometimes a matching base was illuminated from within. Metal mounts were almost invisible and forms strong and sculptural.

Albert Cheuret specialized in unusual and exotic Art Deco lamps, often in animal forms and in a style inspired by Antiquity. Mounts were generally in bronze, and set with thin slices of alabaster. Rateau also produced a range of lamps in bronze which incorporated the highly individual animal motifs that adorned his furniture and interiors.

The lighting of glass, and its potential for decorative effect, was a great stimulus to René Lalique's fantasy and inventiveness. From around 1914 he began to explore the possibilities of lighting glass electrically, and was one of the first to hit upon the idea of suspending a simple shallow bowl or globe from the ceiling. These he molded in characteristic stylized designs – fruit, flowers, fish and birds – which stood out in relief against the diffused glow of the thick opalescent background, most of the light being reflected off the ceiling. Sometimes he added a flattering pastel tint, or colored the glass to harmonize with a particular decor. Often decorative motifs matched wall sconces and even tableware. An extension of the idea of suspending a single basin was to hang a series of basins of decreasing size from the ceiling, one above the other, so that the light thrown upwards from each basin illuminated the moldings or etched decorations of those above. This was an intelligent and effective substitute for the chandelier. Lalique also developed the idea of applying molded glass cornices around a room which concealed electric bulbs and cast an overall diffused light. He used a similar device in his decorative scheme for Maples furniture store in the Tottenham Court Road, London. The firm of Genet and Michon, who specialized in lighting fixtures, were the originators of this idea and manufactured illuminated press-molded glass panels that ran around a room like a cornice or could be placed against walls and ceilings.

Lalique's lighting designs undoubtedly made him more sensitive to the way light could enhance glass: its effect on molding, color, etched decoration and varying thicknesses and textures of glass. He designed a series of *surtouts-de-table*, decorative objects with the light

Right: Glass table lamp with illuminated base, c. 1925, by Daum, one of their innovative range of glass lamps.

Far right: René Lalique's glass chandelier with molded mistletoe design.

Below: Pair of gilt-bronze *La Tentation* floor lamps with Daum shades, early 1920s, by Edgar Brandt.

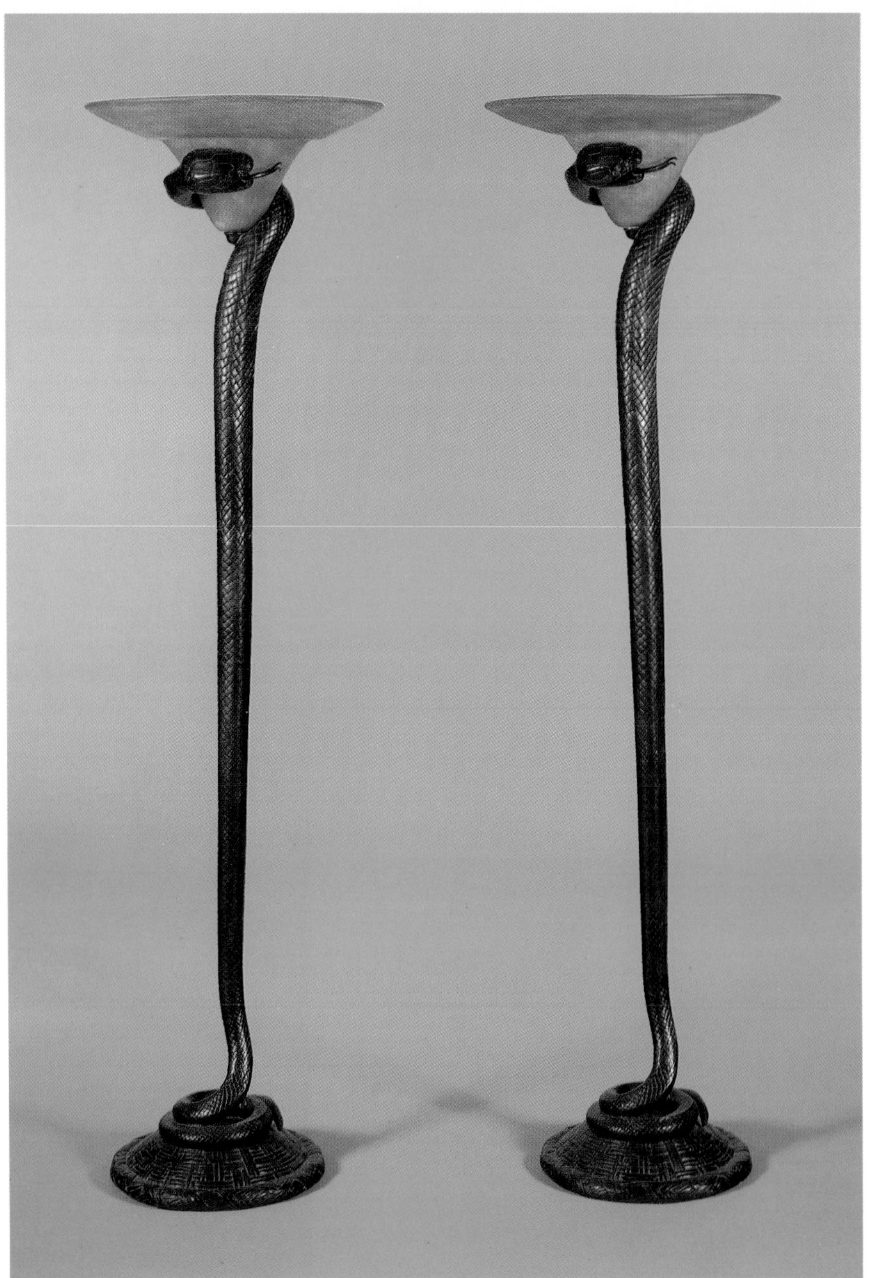

source concealed in a bronze base and thrown upwards on to delicate semicircular sheets of glass etched with peacocks, swallows, or a fire-bird design inspired by Stravinsky's ballet of the same name. These were developed from his glass *luminaires* lamps – illuminated vases sprouting etched bouquets. He also created illuminated ceilings, fountains and tables. Although his glass was never cheap, Lalique designed for large-series production and many of his wares were exported abroad, particularly to England. By the early 1930s his light fittings were almost a cliché of the contemporary interior, in London as much as in Paris.

Ruhlmann designed monumental lighting fixtures and was particularly fond of the urn shape which thrust the light upwards, emphasizing the height of ceilings. He also hung massive chandeliers made up of crystal beads strung together in cascading rivulets. These were quite a feature of the high Deco interior and remained popular through the 1930s. Süe et Mare produced a range of table lamps and wall fixtures, which were most often molded in the flowers-and-fruit relief that adorned so many of their pieces. Many of the artists who worked in *pâte-de-verre*, such as Gabriel Argy-Rousseau and Alméric Walter, produced small sculptured lamps and wall lights in relatively large quantities. The deep colors and translucent quality of the glass made them pretty decorative additions to a room.

Many of the designers who adopted a more modernistic idiom were instrumental in freeing lighting design from its archaic and anachronistic forms and giving it a new importance in decorative schemes. In his capacity both as architect and decorator, Pierre Chareau was particularly sensitive to every aspect of lighting a room. He based his design for the

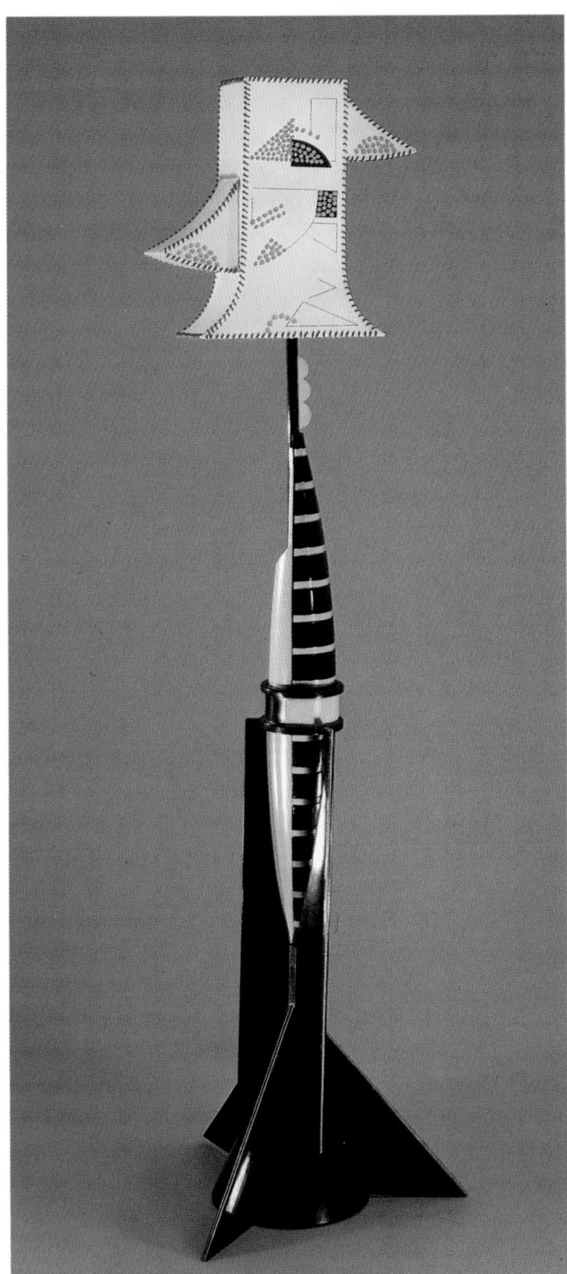

study-library room of the Ambassade Française at the 1925 Exposition around a central cupola, with sliding fan partitions to screen off light. His Maison de Verre of 1928-31, with its entire façade and many of its interior walls made of glass, is a brilliant exercise in filtering the maximum amount of daylight through to an interior without sacrificing a sense of the solidity of the structure and of an enclosed space.

His early lamps were decorative Cubist designs, typified by his standard lamp *'La Religieuse'*, with its conical tapering base and shade made up of triangular sections of alabaster set against one another in an irregular composition. In the early 1920s these designs were adapted to table lamps, wall sconces and ceiling lights. Chareau cleverly contrasted their sharp angles with the diffused glow that filtered from the alabaster slices. He recognized the value of light in softening the rather abrupt planes and forms of Modernist interiors, and favoured alabaster for its extreme translucence. He also used light fixtures to provide decorative interest and to unify large rooms, sometimes creating irregular patterns by scattering numerous small light fixtures across walls and ceilings. The device of using lighting to accentuate architectural features in an interior became very popular with modernistic designers.

Eileen Gray's early lighting designs were very strong and sculptural in conception, and so unusual that they outraged the critics when they were first exhibited. She was concerned with controling the flow of light as well as creating objects that were bold and interesting additions to a room. One ceiling lamp of hers was made up of a metal cylinder fitted at one end with an ostrich egg and pierced irregularly to emit a discreet, softened light. Quite dif-

Above left: Pair of table lamps, 1923, by Waldemar Raemisch; his work combined modernistic and primitive forms.

Above: Pair of lamps in frosted glass and chrome, c. 1928, by Jean Perzel, a technical innovator as well as a brilliant designer.

Left: Eileen Gray's standard lamp with lacquered support and painted parchment shade, 1923.

Above: Jean Perzel's metal and glass lamp shows his mastery of modernistic lighting.

Below: Jacques and Jean Adnet's ceiling lamp in chromed metal with frosted bulbs was marketed by the Compagnie des Arts Français, c. 1930.

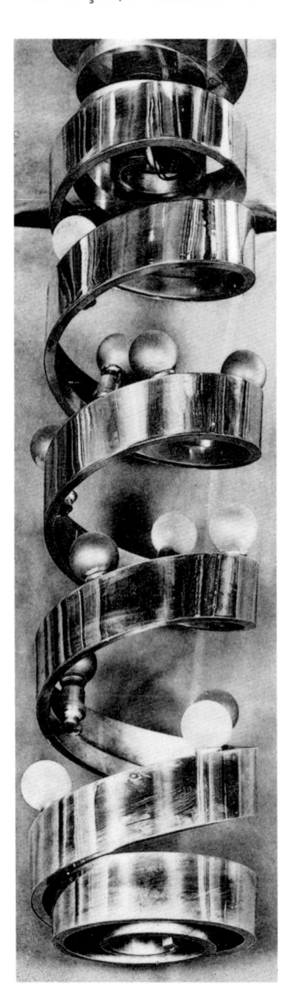

ferent again, and more modernistic in its stylish functionality, simple lines and conical parchment shade, is a floor lamp designed for the Salon des Artistes Décorateurs of 1923. Her parchment lampshades with appliquéd geometrical designs were perhaps the origin of the fashion that appeared much later in the 1930s for applying painted jazz motifs to parchment shades.

Many of the lamps designed by the more avant-garde artists were conceived as Cubist-type sculptures. Most of Eileen Gray's early lamps incorporate a Cubist treatment of forms and motifs. Jean Goulden created enameled table lamps and night lights which, like his clocks, were built up of juxtaposed planes, shapes and colors. The light source was embedded in the stand and treated as another decorative element in the design, set against the enamel and metal. Jean Lambert-Rucki sculpted elaborate bases for lamps in a style inspired by Cubism and African tribal art. These were usually crowned with a simple parchment shade. For the Deutsche Werkbund the painter and sculptor Waldemar Raemisch designed figural bronze table lamps in an individual style, a cross between modernistic machined and primitive forms.

Under the influence of Modernism, lighting became more functional and the pairing of metal and glass, so beloved of modernistic designers, began to predominate. With the general fashion for clean, bare and well-lit interiors, lighting was stripped of its silk shades, its thick moldings, its dim diffused quality, and became the focus of a search for clarity and maximum efficiency. Attention turned to the light source as prime element in the design, and lamps ceased to masquerade apologetically as *objets d'art*. Improvements in the manufacture of glass made it possible to cast glass in finer sections and therefore to produce a stronger light source. Globes or simple shapes in frosted glass that radiated an even light became fashionable. These forms were carefully constructed and joined with tiny metal armatures, so that the seams were virtually invisible. A simple chromed metal stand, cylindrical or spherical, and wide conical shade either in parchment, frosted glass or similar translucent material was also popular. Lights were frequently set into walls and ceilings, disposing of the need for fixtures and sconces. But the decorative potential of lighting was never quite forgotten. René Herbst used lighting in a particularly sensitive way; his lighting designs were always delicate, stylish and unusual, giving a flourish to his over-orderly and even characterless interiors.

The Bauhaus artist Marianne Brandt turned from metalwork to lighting and devised functional lighting fixtures including the famous Kandem bedside light with push-button switch and adjustable reflector, which became a prototype for bedside lamps worldwide.

Jean Perzel was the master of modernistic lighting, a brilliant technician as well as an imaginative designer. He was a Czech who first came to Paris in 1910 to develop the technique of glass window decoration. From 1923 onward he specialized in lighting. His early experiments display an interest in improving the quality and distribution of light that was to dominate his career. He was fascinated by electricity and was concerned to present light in the best possible form, both from an aesthetic and a functional point of view. He investigated the psychological effect of good and bad lighting in an interior, recognizing that the brilliantly lit Modernist interior was rather too functional for comfort and ease. At first he used colorless glass in his designs, sandblasted and enameled to a restful degree of opacity so that the light filtered through evenly and was bright, but not too bright. Equally he sought to give rational form to the lighting device. His early designs did not eliminate the points of light formed by the bulb, and this led him to create overlapping geometrical shapes: disks, cylinders or a build-up of semi-cylinders, always devoid of ornament. Mounts were always minimal but by the early 1930s they were sometimes completely invisible, and fittings were reduced to simple geometrical shapes resembling sculptured light. His glass was mainly colorless; sometimes he added pinkish tints that cast a flattering glow, or hints of color to harmonize with a decor. Perzel held that lighting should not reduce an interior to an evenly illuminated box, but should take into account the play of shadows and reflected light. His polished metal shades and fitments were intended to reflect light.

Like Perzel, Boris Lacroix contributed intelligent designs to the field of lighting. He emphasized the role of metal, often using polished steel and nickel surfaces as light reflectors. His forms were simple and geometrical. Georges Lechevallier-Chevignard created stark machined forms from flat planes of metal, exposing the rivets and leaving the metal unpolished to create surface interest.

Equally bold in their way were the designs of the Adnet brothers, who were strongly influenced by Le Corbusier and were responsible for introducing the Modernist philosophy of truth to materials and simplicity of design to the field of lighting. They designed fixtures that flaunted bare bulbs, and exhibited a spectacular range of zigzagged tubular glass lights at the 1925 Exposition.

The Maison Desny was established around 1927, providing a complete range of furnishings in a smart, Cubist-inspired, geometrical style. Their lighting designs, illuminated sculptures in polished chrome and opaque glass, were clever and sophisticated constructions. Smart inexpensive fixtures in up-to-the-minute geometrical designs, often made of the early mottled plastic, were common in the late 1920s and 1930s.

In Britain lighting was used in hotels, restaurants, night clubs and cinemas to create dramatic Hollywood-style effects. The results range from merely gimmicky to strong and spectacular. Designers dreamt up multi-bulb fixtures, starburst designs and illuminated panels. Upwardly directed lighting combined with decorative molding on a ceiling created a dramatic effect suitable for important entranceways; the best extant example of this can be seen in the foyer of the *Daily Express* building in London.

Left: Chromed metal and glass table lamp, late 1920s, by Maison Desny.

Below: Entrance to the Strand Palace Hotel, London, 1930s.

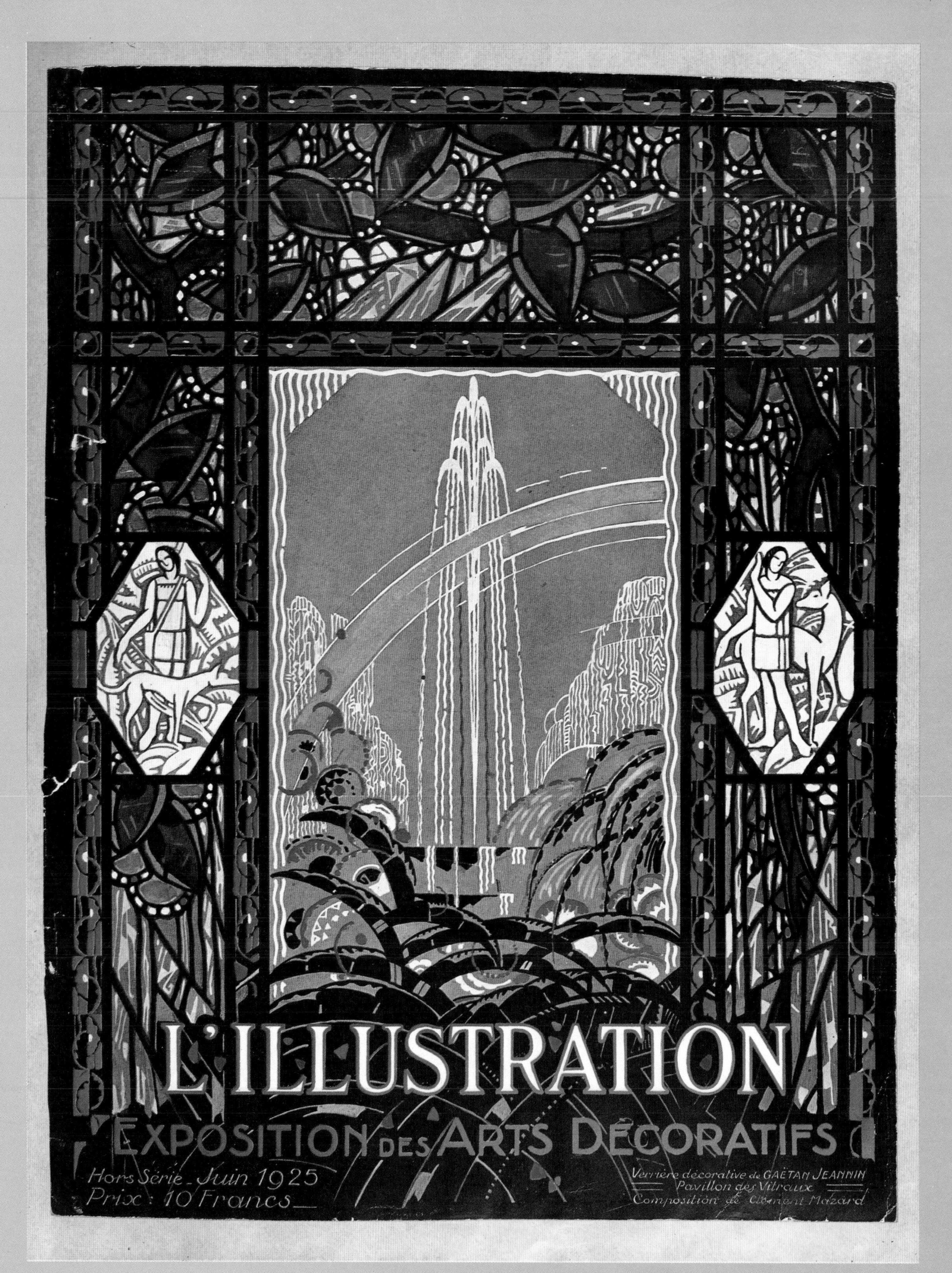
L'ILLUSTRATION
EXPOSITION DES ARTS DÉCORATIFS
Hors Série _ Juin 1925
Prix : 10 Francs
Verrière décorative de GAËTAN JEANNIN
Pavillon des Vitraux
Composition de Clément Mazard

6
GLASS

Opposite: Gaetan Jeannin's design for a stained glass window, *Le Jet d'Eau,* was used for the cover of a special publication on the 1925 Exposition.

From René Lalique, who developed techniques of mass-producing high quality glassware, to Maurice Marinot, who revised methods of handworking glass, the Art Deco period is characterized by a great variety of treatments and decorative effects in glass design. Glassworkers gained a degree of technical mastery of the material that gave them a new freedom in design and allowed them to break completely with past styles. In the latter half of the period, glass attained a status it had never enjoyed before, and its uses and applications multiplied.

The story of the modernization of glass really begins with the Art Nouveau *maîtres verriers* – Emile Gallé, Eugène Rousseau and Dammouse – who revived craftsmanlike techniques and pioneered new ones. The best of the glassworkers who succeeded them continued to focus on materials and methods of production as a means of creating a strong modern style of glassware.

Pâte-de-verre had been popular with Art Nouveau glassworkers, and came back into vogue during the 1920s and 1930s. It is made by mixing finely ground glass with a fluxing agent. The resultant paste is colored by adding metallic oxides or granules of colored glass, molded or modeled into the desired form, and then fired at a high temperature. The colors fuse into one another, and the glass takes on a jewel-like translucent quality with a slightly waxy surface rather like soapstone. *Pâte-de-verre's* brilliant color effects distinguish it from other glass of the interwar period, much of which was either monochrome or clear.

Below: *Pâte-de-verre* vase by Gabriel Argy-Rousseau.

François-Emile Décorchemont and Joseph-Gabriel Argy-Rousseau were the two great Art Deco *pâte-de-verre* artists. Décorchemont's work of the first decade of the century was in the Art Nouveau style, highly decorative and modeled in opaque, brittle glass that closely resembled enamel, but around 1910 he had begun to concentrate on creating larger forms. Bold, thick-walled vessels, streaked and swirled with color to evoke the mottled effect of antique glass, marble or other hardstones are characteristic of this later style. Color continued to be an important element in Décorchemont's work and he developed a range of brilliant and unusual hues, including a semi-translucent golden brown resembling tortoiseshell. The shapes of his vessels became more geometrical and handles were often emphasized, sometimes designed in the form of stylized animals, while the vessels themselves were decorated with flowers and fruit. In the late 1920s forms were simplified still further and became more angular, often molded in imitation of carved stone and still in the jewel-like colors of his earlier work. By the mid-1930s he had shifted his interest to the creation of large panels in *pâte-de-verre*, a richer, more opaque alternative to leaded glass.

Argy-Rousseau also made *pâte-de-verre* his speciality and set up a company to manufacture his extensive range of decorative objects, each item individually colored and finished. Much of his work was lightweight and opaque, decorated with flowers and animals and often displaying the lingering influence of Art Nouveau glassware. But he is better known for his designs in *pâte-de-cristal* (the addition of lead enriched and clarified the colors) which were molded with neoclassical motifs. He developed a more angular geometrical style in the late 1920s and 1930s, creating chunky vases and bowls that were swirled or streaked with translucent color.

Another group of glassworkers of this period were exploring the rich color effects and clarity of definition of enameled glass. Marcel Goupy was an important exponent of this technique, and his assistant Auguste-Claude Heiligenstein became a notable enamelist in his own right. The crisp quality of enamel was particularly suited to Art Deco stylizations. Goupy specialized in a high Deco repertoire of birds, flowers, animals and figurative designs – female nudes and mythological figures – which he painted onto the surfaces of his glass vessels in brightly colored enamels. He produced mostly decorative ware, although he did design some cleverly co-ordinated tableware in glass and ceramic.

The Daum company of Nancy made its name at the end of the nineteenth century with a successful range of Art Nouveau glassware in the style of Emile Gallé. In 1919 the company reopened, producing a range of simple geometrical vessels that were internally colored with swirls of metal oxides, or overlays of gold, silver or platinum foils which broke up into a multitude of tiny specks. Sometimes this glass was blown into iron armatures by Edgar Brandt, or used to make shades for his lampstands. No doubt Daum was influenced by the thick-walled, heavily textured style of Maurice Marinot's work when, in the mid-1920s, they developed a style characterized by deeply etched angular designs on a simple, chunky, glass form and typically colored in greens, blues and oranges. Standard Deco motifs of geometricized fruit, flowers and abstract patterns were etched away in relief with acid, so that the design stood out smooth-surfaced against a rough-textured background.

Schneider, among other companies, took to etching their vessels and produced a range of cheerful and elegant colored glass that was lightly patterned in Deco-style geometrical designs. They also produced a range of glassware in mottled marblized colors. Jean Luce achieved similar contrasts of rough and smooth by sand-blasting geometrical decorations onto plain forms, and sometimes applied mirrored or gilded finishes in abstract geometrical patterns.

The highly versatile and talented René Lalique abandoned his career as a successful Art Nouveau jeweler to become a brilliant *maître verrier* working in the high Art Deco style. He first used glass in his jewelry designs and began making glass experimentally as early as 1890. The year 1908 really marks his switch to glasswork, when he was commissioned by the *parfumiers* Coty to design scent bottles and packaging. From that time on Lalique concentrated increasingly on glass design, taking over first a glassworks and then later a larger workshop, where he could apply industrial techniques of production and therefore mass produce his wares and reduce costs. The new medium absorbed him totally and by around 1915 he had almost ceased designing jewelry.

Lalique tended to work in *demi-cristal*, glass with a 50 percent lead content. The quality both of design and production was consistently high, so much so that many of his pieces seem too exquisite to be made of mere glass. He was a technical wizard, endlessly experimenting with different methods of achieving contrasting finishes: frosting with acids; enameling and staining to accent relief molding; exposing glass to a mixture of gases to produce an antiquated patina; buffing the glass to polish it. By sandwiching opaque glass between layers of colorless glass, he achieved wonderful opalescent effects that softened the *demi-cristal* and gave it an unearthly, lunar quality. His early designs were influenced by Art Nouveau but by around 1913 he had developed a style that was rational and harmonious; forms were simple, decorated in molded relief with female nudes, birds, fish, fruit, flowers and other motifs drawn from nature. Most of his output was in this graceful classical style, but he also designed some streamlined modernistic pieces in the late 1920s, including a series of

Above: Victoire, molded glass car mascot, 1929, by René Lalique, an example of his streamlined modernistic style.

Below: François-Emile Décorchemont's *pâte-de-verre* bowl, 1920s.

Right: Mottled glass vase enameled with classical figures, c. 1925, by Marcel Goupy.

Below: Acid-etched blue glass vase, 1930s, by the Daum company.

car mascots, and some of his naturalistic forms were rendered in a near-abstract fashion. Usually the glass was blown mechanically or by mouth into prepared molds, or cast in a stamping press. From the mid-1920s Lalique made a few unique pieces using the *cire perdue* method adapted from bronze casting; a model carved in wax was covered in clay, the wax was melted out and replaced with molten glass. These were in a different category from his commercial output and were subtly textured, often even marked with his own fingerprints.

By the end of his career Lalique had virtually exhausted the applications of glass, and his repertoire included sculpture and ornamental pieces, tableware, vases, toiletry items, jewelry, clock cases, light fixtures, mirrors, tables, fountains and architectural fittings. The last included panels for London's Claridge's Hotel and, probably his most spectacular architectural assignment, the first-class dining room for the liner *Normandie*, with vast chandeliers and illuminated light panels, glass panels covering the walls and an illuminated coffered ceiling. His numerous lighting designs reflect his sensitivity to the play of light on glass, and particularly on etched and relief surfaces. Lalique exhibited widely at the 1925 Exposition, to great critical acclaim. His style was enormously popular, particularly during the 1920s and

Left: Glass vase by Daum, blown into a wrought-iron frame by Majorelle.

Below: René Lalique's grasshopper vase, an early design from c. 1920.

1930s, and was much imitated, both in France and abroad.

While Lalique used industrial methods to mass produce his work, Maurice Marinot emphasized the craft aspect of glasswork and each of his pieces was handworked and unique. Marinot was largely responsible for the change in direction that glass design took during this period. The decorative possibilities, the techniques, the materials, the forms, all were entirely rethought and the results were utterly new. He combined craftsmanlike techniques with an accumulated knowledge of the properties of glass. His output was relatively small and each piece was laboriously and painstakingly crafted.

Marinot began his career as a painter and was associated with the Fauves school, but a visit to the glassworks of some friends inspired him to train as a glassworker and he began gradually to make experiments of his own. By 1913 he was concentrating almost exclusively on glass design. His first essays consisted of figurative decoration, rather painterly in style, which he applied in bright enamels. His interest in developing new techniques led him to experiment with ways of creating enamels that were translucent rather than opaque, and methods of layering the enamel so that it integrated with the glass. In the early 1920s he abandoned

Right: Carved and chiseled glass vase, late 1920s, by Aristide Colotte, who specialized in sculptural effects.

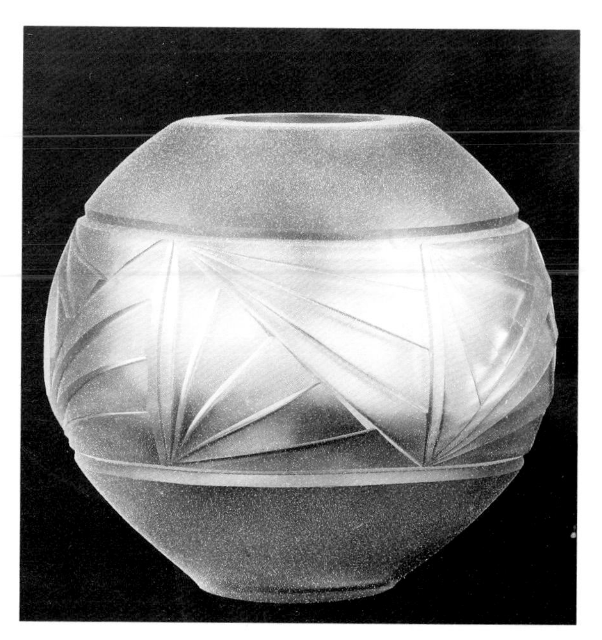

Far right: Carved and frosted glass vase by Aristide Colotte.

superficially applied decoration altogether and began to blow his own glass vessels and work the mass of the glass into sculptural forms while it was still hot, exploiting qualities inherent in the material and faults in composition to create abstract decorative effects. He would allow air bubbles to form and trap them between layers of clear glass; apply internal whirls and streaks of color; tease out impurities in the glass; or apply chemicals for crackled effects. Generally a smooth outer surface provided contrast to the internal texture. He also produced more dynamic sculptural effects by repeated bathing in hydrofluoric acid, which etched away at thick glass vessels in crude geometrical relief; many of these pieces resemble blocks of melted ice. Later still he worked vessels at the furnace, modeling and carving directly into the glass or building up a piece with numerous applications of molten glass, again for massive sculptural effects. Sometimes he applied primitive mask designs in molten glass. His vessels are thick-walled and massive and bottles are crowned with tiny spherical stoppers. Basic forms are simple ovoid, cylindrical and spherical gourd shapes. Marinot went on working in glass until the late 1930s. His work found recognition early on and most of his pieces were quickly bought up by museums. He had many imitators, and exercised a considerable influence on glass design of the interwar years in France and elsewhere in Europe, liberating it from conventional treatments. Henri Navarre was his greatest follower, and continued to develop Marinot's techniques of internal decoration (with powdered oxides, streaks and bubbles) and of working at the kiln, though in a style more elaborate than Marinot's and often in crystal rather than glass.

Below: This glass vase with three girls was designed by Vicke Lindstrand for Orrefors.

Aristide Colotte also favored largescale sculptural effects, but his method was to carve and chisel at the glass. In his mature phase he executed some extremely forceful, purely abstract pieces, but he never entirely abandoned figurative and animal themes. Sometimes he carved glass figures at the wheel and etched away at blocks of raw glass or crystal, creating highly polished and rough finishes that generate an interesting play of light.

In the wake of Lalique's success, derivative molded glass was produced all over Europe, particularly in Italy, England and in France itself. There was also, however, much innovation in modern glass design throughout

Left: Louis Barillet's stained glass window wall in the Bally shoe store in Paris. The architect responsible for the design of the new shoe store was Robert Mallet-Stevens, who collaborated with Barillet on a number of projects.

Europe. A number of designers attached to the Wiener Werkstätte produced modern glassware; Hoffmann, Moser and Dagobert Peche were the most notable. In Denmark, Finland and the Netherlands there were companies producing everyday and art glass in the modern idiom, and they often drew their inspiration from the immense creative output of the French glassworkers.

Glassworkers in Sweden earned a high reputation in this period, particularly those of the Orrefors factory, who developed a style similar in spirit to but not derivative of French design. During World War I a campaign had been launched by the Swedish Society of Industrial Design based on the ideas of Hermann Muthesius, with the aim of encouraging the application of good design to industry. The Orrefors company was one of the first to take advantage of this new union of art with industry. Simon Gate and Edward Hald were employed to initiate the scheme. Gate chose to investigate the cameo technique (a design was acid-etched on to a vessel, fused at the furnace and then sandwiched in clear glass and polished), which was characteristic of Art Nouveau and Emile Gallé's work, out of which he developed the Graal technique (layers of glass were etched or carved with relief decoration and these images were fused in the furnace). Hald on the other hand, who had studied under Matisse in Paris, introduced a more modernistic element into the firm's design. Both Gate and Hald executed a good deal of mainly figurative wheel-engraved decoration. In the late 1920s they were joined by Edvin Ohrström and Vicke Lindstrand, who contributed a forceful Modernist element to the Orrefors output. Ohrström developed a variation of the Graal technique, which involved trapping patterns of air bubbles in a case of clear glass and which he called the Ariel technique. The Orrefors exhibits at the 1925 Exposition received great acclaim and influenced designers throughout Europe.

Czechoslovakia had long been renowned for its glassware and produced a range of bold

Below: Glass dressing table and stool, 1933, by Oliver Hill for Pilkington Glass.

Right: Glass vase, wheel-cut with vertical and horizontal grooves, 1937, by Keith Murray for Stevens and Williams.

Cubist-inspired wares. Equally sophisticated Deco glassware was coming out of Germany and Belgium. In Britain, however, traditional glass designs predominated and the output of the 1920s and 1930s was notably uninspired and lacking in quality. In general cheap, well-designed glassware was imported from abroad. Some decorative glass was produced in imitation of French and Swedish styles, but the best work in the Modernist idiom was done by the New Zealander Keith Murray, who was also an architect and a designer of silver and ceramics. His interest in designing glass stemmed from a deep admiration for eighteenth-century English glass and was further stimulated by his visit to the 1925 Exposition, where he saw the Swedish, and particularly the Orrefors exhibit, and also admired the Finnish and Czechoslovakian glass. He began designing glassware in 1931 for Stevens and Williams of Brierley Hill, Staffordshire. For Murray form was supremely important –

Right: René Lalique: *Trépied Sirène* bowl, made of opalescent glass with molded design and raised on three low feet.

teriors such as theatre foyers and hotels. Mirror too became a fashionable material and enjoyed the same variety of applications; furniture, walls, floors, even clocks and boxes were mirrored.

Verre églomisé panels (glass painted and highlighted in gold and silver leaf on the reverse) were popular as largescale lavish and decorative murals. The most famous was the series of panels designed by Jean Dupas for the French ocean liner *Normandie*, depicting the history of navigation.

A few artists devoted themselves to modernizing techniques of staining glass and other aspects of the craft. Jacques Gruber designed figurative compositions in an angular 1920s style, while Louis Barillet worked in a strictly geometrical idiom and a restricted range of colors, mainly tones of gray, white and black. He worked frequently with Mallet-Stevens and designed leaded glass friezes for his Pavillon de Tourisme at the 1925 Exposition.

Left: Hand-blown flask and stopper, 1929, by Maurice Marinot.

Below: Maurice Marinot's engraved, stoppered bottle with interior decoration; a more tactile, eye-catching design than the classic example above.

decoration was often minimal, consisting simply of a little machined fluting, and colors were restrained, although he did also design more decorative pieces, some with jazzy enameled motifs, others with engraved Swedish-style designs.

In Italy Venini revived the stultified glass industry of Venice, which had been endlessly repeating the designs of its sixteenth-century heyday, with smart, scarcely ornamented pieces and experiments with color and texture. A visit to the 1925 Exposition generated a number of interesting interpretations of the Art Deco theme by various Italian glassworkers.

The importance and range of uses of glass increased throughout the 1920s, and by the end of the decade it enjoyed the status of 'material of the moment', alongside aluminum, steel and concrete. Glass became associated with light, cleanliness, purity and hygiene: all the qualities of modern living. The Modernists (particularly the Bauhaus artists) did much to exalt glass and to expand its applications and uses, most notably in the field of architecture. In 1920 Mies Van der Rohe designed a skyscraper entirely clad in glass. Architects such as Chareau and Mallet-Stevens took up the glass theme and made innovative use of it in their own designs. The façade of Chareau's Maison de Verre of 1928-31 was made entirely of glass bricks and panels, and most of the internal partitions were glass too. Glass, as well as being practical and hygenic was chic – hard, glossy and smooth – and as such was appealing as a furnishing material. Coffered glass ceilings, paneled glass walls and glass tiles on the floor were the height of chic and sophistication in the late 1920s and early 1930s, especially if illuminated. Illuminated wall paneling was particularly suited to spectacular and grand in-

7
SILVER

Opposite: *Flèche* candlestick, 1933, by Gio Ponti for Christofle.

Silver is not a metal usually associated with innovative or avant-garde design. Because of its value it has always been reserved for luxury objects, and designs for silverware have tended to be of the most conservative and traditional type. This was particularly true of the early twentieth century, when Art Deco was beginning to permeate the decorative arts. It was chiefly thanks to the brilliant technical and design skills of Jean Puiforcat that silverware made so successful a transition from tradition to modernity. Not only was he the best silversmith of the period, he also ranked among the best of all Art Deco designers. Along with a handful of other silversmiths he showed that designs for silverware could be brought up to date in an elegant and dignified fashion. In their wake the manufacturers of silverware began tentatively to contribute modern designs, and silverware slowly followed the evolution of the other decorative arts.

Like gold, silver is a soft and malleable metal and can be worked in a variety of ways. Forms can be rendered either by cutting, casting or hammering. Most of the best Deco silversmiths made use of the new techniques of stamping, spinning and casting silver but finished the pieces by hand. The laborious technique of hammering the metal was not used for commercial production. After the 1929 Wall Street crash, the demand for silverware virtually ceased and plated metals became increasingly common. Some firms would offer versions of the same design in both solid and plated silver.

Puiforcat's family were goldsmiths and he began his career by serving as an apprentice in his father's firm, before going on to study sculpture for a time. He exhibited his first designs at the Salon d'Automne of 1921. By the following year the Musée des Arts Décoratifs had bought one of his pieces, and his genius was confirmed.

From the first Puiforcat's designs were innovative. He eschewed surface ornament altogether and concentrated on simplifying form to its most functional and minimal. The task he set himself was not by any means a simple one, for the silver could easily appear dull and lifeless without its habitual surface embellishments. Only by studying the properties and qualities of the metal in relation to design was he able to create pieces that were restrained and elegant, and yet at the same time played on the rich tonal effects of the metal. His work is absolutely unembellished; surfaces are as smooth and shiny as satin and bear none of the hammer marks of traditional handmade silverware. These smooth planes are built up into

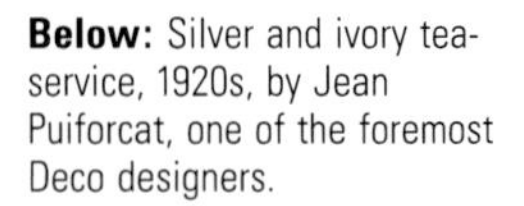

Below: Silver and ivory tea-service, 1920s, by Jean Puiforcat, one of the foremost Deco designers.

Left: Jean Puiforcat's silver flatware service, 1920s.

Below: Jean Puiforcat's silver and onyx clock, c. 1932, illustrates his interest in geometrical harmony.

beautifully proportioned forms. A clever device he used to enliven his designs was to facet a piece almost imperceptibly, so that reflected light was thrown off at different angles. Like the best glassworkers, he understood the importance of manipulating the play of light on surfaces. He also discovered that certain rare woods or semi-precious stones, incorporated as handles and finials, successfully complemented a simple form and added to the play of reflections and tones, as well as emphasizing textural contrasts.

Platonic ideals of simplicity and harmony govern the design of Puiforcat's pieces. All his forms are derived from basic geometrical shapes and relate to each other according to arithmetical proportions. Beyond being functional, a piece had to be as graceful as he was able to make it. His perfectly executed designs on paper bear witness to a meticulous and highly organized method of design, based on three fundamental shapes; the sphere, cone and cylinder. His output included many coffee and tea services, liturgical pieces, flatware and candlesticks, table lamps, even chess sets in silver, ivory and ebony – all supremely elegant pieces, often embellished with lapis-lazuli, crystal, tinted glass, ebony or ivory. His tableware is equally understated and plain, at most ornamented with a little discreet fluting or banding.

Puiforcat was a founder member of the Union des Artistes Modernes, which was formed in 1930. Like other members of the UAM, he worked in a pared-down style that

Right: Christian Fjerdlingstad's *Cygne*, or Swan sauce boat, 1933.

aimed to unify design and function, but he did not embrace Modernist ideals of mass production. He believed in principle in the dissemination of good design through industry, but felt that he himself could not mass produce his own designs without loss of quality.

Another silversmith responsible for the rejuvenation of silver design was Jean Tétard. His firm, Tétard *frères*, was one of the few that chose not to cling to tradition but to introduce a bold modern style for functional tableware. His work displays great technical virtuosity; forms are complex but also largely undecorated, generally with handles carved in rich rare woods.

A number of noted Art Deco designers created modernistic silverware for the Parisian firm Christofle, which was one of the most advanced of the large firms selling metalwork. They included Gio Ponti, the pewtersmith

Below: 'Cube' tea service by Charles Boyton, c. 1930.

Left: Silver vegetable dish by the Danish silversmith Georg Jensen, an example of his plainer more modernistic style.

Maurice Daurat, André Groult, Paul Follot and Christian Fjerdlingstad. Christofle purchased most of the patents for the electroplating system of silver plating which was developed in the nineteenth century, and during the Art Deco period produced a good deal of electroplated tableware. One of the few large firms producing silverware in the Art Deco style, they were very successul and marketed abroad in London, Vienna, and in America. Gio Ponti's designs for silver are characteristically elegant, with sleek and tapering forms, while the Dane Christian Fjerdlingstad worked in an elegant minimalist style.

Süe et Mare's great dominion extended over silverware too, and Louis Süe designed both for his own Compagnie des Arts Français and for Christofle. His pieces are elegantly shaped, based on traditional forms, and faceted in the Cubist manner. Süe et Mare also designed some silverware in their characteristically elaborate decorative manner.

The jeweler Jean Desprès created very plain objects in silver that were often rather angular and exaggeratedly Cubist in treatment. His surfaces are unornamented but hammered to a rough texture, to create a lively play of light and tone, rather than smooth and shiny. He made no attempt to disguise bolts and rivets but incorporated them into his designs as 'decoration'. Shapes were deliberately fashioned to resemble machine parts. Another jeweler and independent craftsman, Gérard Sandoz, produced a number of refined and unusual silver objects which he embellished with sumptuous materials like shagreen, lizard skin and ivory. He too hammered the metal to create a textured finish and flaunted bolts and rivets. Unlike Puiforcat's pieces, these often aggressively modernistic designs can now seem rather clumsy and dated.

The Parisian firm Desny produced more sophisticated, modernistic silverware for a fashionable clientele – their sleek conical cocktail sets were particularly popular. Many of their pieces were silver-plated and therefore not prohibitive in price.

Below: Box in silver and ivory by Charles Boyton, c. 1930.

Opposite above Coffee and tea service in silver with wooden handles, c. 1924, by the Bauhaus designer Marianne Brandt.

Opposite below: Silver cigarette box with turned ivory finial, 1938, by the English silversmith H. G. Murphy.

During this period much ingenuity was employed in the design of clocks. Now that clocks could be run by electricity they did not need to be so large and cumbersome, nor did they need to be strategically placed for easy winding. Clock design therefore offered a relatively unconstrained opportunity for the artist to display his creative and innovative talents. Art Deco clocks range in style from tiny and jewel-like, through floral and fussy, to rigorous and modernistic examples. Designs are often quirky or eccentric but the best are also exciting and unusual. One of the most interesting clocks of the period is a minimalist arrangement of numerals, hands and base in silver designed by Puiforcat. Melik Minassiantz invented a clock that had no hands, but indicated the time by a system of balls rotating in circular grooves. Albert Cheuret is best known for his lighting devices, but he also designed a number of clocks in silvered bronze, most notable of which is his clock styled in the Egyptian mode with Egyptian numerals and Egyptian headdress surround.

At the same time there was quite a vogue for rather gimmicky compact silver tea services, the various elements designed to fit together to make up an amusing and unusual display, although the individual pieces, being so rigidly geometrical, were not always terribly functional. Boris Lacroix, Desny, Gérard Sandoz and Charles Boyton all designed variations on this compact cubic theme, often with matching trays.

In England a design for a teapot compacted into a cube shape was introduced in the early 1920s. By the late 1920s and 1930s it was available both in ceramic and silver and had become widely popular, despite the fact that the spouts were ineffective and the handles could not be properly grasped. Much of the modern silverware in Britain was in this very angular style, reflecting the quest for novelty and modernity.

The Bauhaus artist Marianne Brandt was a metalworker before she turned to lighting design. In the 1920s she designed some fine silver pieces, many of them based on an interesting play of curves. These were far more elegant and less austere than the majority of silver and metalware designs coming out of the Bauhaus at this time.

Georg Jensen was a Danish silversmith whose firm, based in Copenhagen, produced a

Below: Silver-plated cocktail set, 1920s, by the Maison Desny, typical of their simple elegant style.

wide range of goods in silver. His firm sold silverware in a variety of styles, including an elaborate high Deco characterized by its decorative scrolls, flowers and leaves, as well as a more modernistic, plain style. Jensen himself had a powerful influence on silver design of the period. He was notable for making many of his pieces accessible to the growing middle classes by producing relatively inexpensive silverware. He had a number of designers working for him, but was a formidable designer himself. He developed a style in the 1920s that was elegant and modernistic but not utterly plain, for he frequently used little silver beads as a decorative device. Sometimes he set his pieces with semi-precious stones.

The architect Harald Nielsen also worked for Jensen, contributing a functionalist style that was influenced by the Bauhaus. He was famous for his 'pyramid' cutlery design.

Jensen's fame spread as he began to open branches around Europe – first in Berlin in 1908, then in Paris in 1919, in London in 1920 and a little later in New York and Stockholm.

The development of silver design in England in the 1920s was held back by the dominance of the Arts and Crafts style. Charles Boyton was one of the few who broke away from the Arts and Crafts manner. He worked in a strong angular style and favored compact shapes and the use of fine woods and ivory for handles and finials. Other silversmiths incorporated stylized floral and geometrical motifs in the Parisian manner. H G Murphy created a series of boxes with plain bodies and elaborate finials, often incorporating exotic materials like coral and ivory.

8
JEWELRY

Opposite: Van Cleef and Arpels's 'mystery' clock – a jade bear on a base of black onyx supporting a crystal disk set with rose-cut diamonds, 1930s.

Art Deco craftsmen broke with traditional styles of jewelry, as well as conventions as to how it should be worn, but they owed much to Art Nouveau jewelers who had already wrought considerable changes; their use of non-precious and semi-precious materials in conjunction with precious stones and metals was particularly inspiring to the jewelers of the interwar period, setting a high standard of inventiveness and creativity which was emulated by their successors. Tortoiseshell, ivory, mother-of-pearl, enamel, lacqueur and glass were all materials introduced by Art Nouveau and exploited by Art Deco jewelers.

Although there were a few adherents of the Deco style in jewelry outside France, more so after the 1925 Exposition, Paris remained the center of the great surge of creativity in jewelry design. Long-established firms such as Mauboussin, Cartier and Boucheron still dominated the jewelry scene and successfully adapted to the Deco style; Louis Cartier, Raymond Templier, Jean Fouquet and Gérard Sandoz were all grandsons of the men who had founded their respective firms. These firms used their own in-house designers as well as buying or commissioning designs from independent artists.

The vibrant colors that began to dominate the decorative arts before World War I sent jewelry designers in search of new materials to add to those introduced by the Art Nouveau jewelers. Striking contrasts were created, with diamonds and other precious stones and metals set against the smooth surfaces and uniform color of hardstones such as coral, jade, black and white onyx, lapis lazuli, turquoise, amber and malachite. Mauboussin were particularly renowned for their colorful jewelry.

Diamonds never really go out of fashion but they were given a fresh lease of life during this period, thanks to a Dutch diamond-cutting firm outside Paris which devised new ways of faceting stones. Their *baguette* cut – the diamond cut into a thin faceted rectangular form – set against diamonds or gemstones of other cuts, created an almost Cubist juxtaposition of planes and forms, and luminous effects of refracted light. The *baguette* cut was a notable feature of jewelry design from the early 1920s. Diamonds were traditionally the focal point of a piece of jewelry but were not always so prominently displayed in this period. They were often used to highlight the lines of a piece, or juxtaposed with other gemstones and hardstones to create interesting color combinations.

The display of technical virtuosity was an important feature of jewelry design of the period. Jewelers took pride in creating invisible settings and flexible structures for stones; bracelets and necklaces resembled ribbons of pure color. Platinum was a recent discovery and became popular. It was easy to work but immensely strong, enabling jewelers to set stones almost invisibly in open-claw settings, rather than the traditional metal cup. The light platinum mounts allowed light to pass through transparent stones, thus showing them to far better advantage than previously. Pearls were widely used, chiefly because they were now available in large numbers through the new method of culturing devised by the Japanese Mikimoto. Rock crystal was admired for its limpid quality, as well as for its velvety matt surface when frosted, and was used a good deal in composite jewelry designs.

Jewelry design showed a marked tendency to simplification and stylization, and motifs

Below: Earrings in gold, ivory and enamel, rings in yellow and white gold, coral, carnelian and onyx, all c. 1925, by Raymond Templier.

Below right: Boucheron's drop earrings in jade, onyx and diamonds, 1920s.

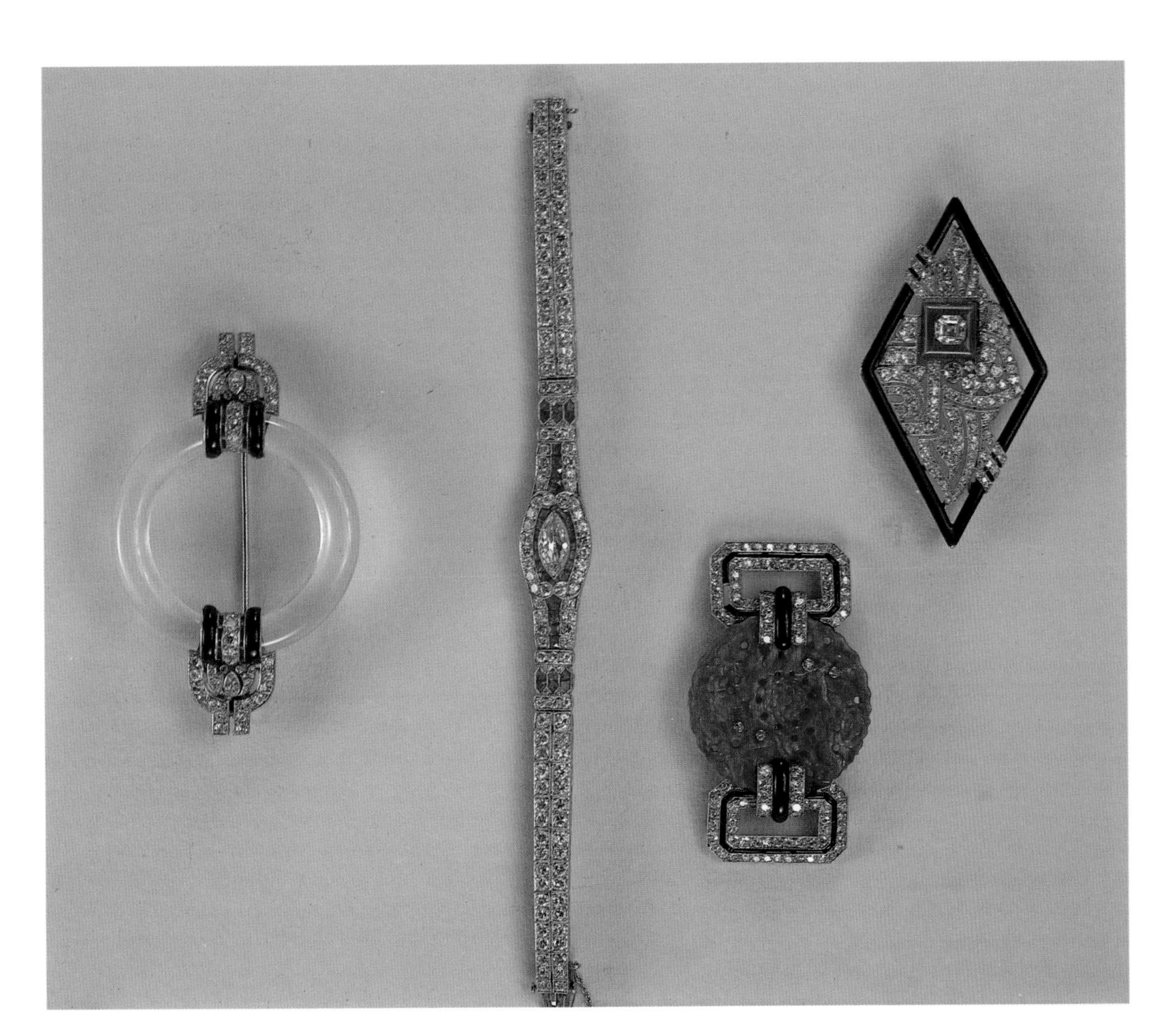

Left: Boucheron's diamond jewelry, c. 1925, displays technical virtuosity applied to a traditional stone.

ranged from stylized figurative to geometric abstraction. Elaborate multicolored clusters of gemstones, skilfully worked into leaf, fruit or flower shapes to form brooches, buckles, rings and pendants, were popular. The stylized flower basket, so typical of Art Deco design, was a motif common to jewelry too. Many designers drew on a knowledge of the foreign art forms that inspired Art Deco, in particular those of the Orient. The firms of Cartier and Lacloche specialized in Oriental-style accessories and jewelry. Materials such as jade, coral, lacquer and enamel were used for their color, and jade and coral were frequently carved with Chinese motifs. The Egyptian craze that followed the discovery of Tutankhamun's tomb in 1922 was reflected as much in jewelry design as in the other decorative arts, while the colonial exhibitions of 1922 and 1931 helped to initiate a vogue for carved African jewelry that reached its height in the 1930s.

The developments in women's fashion of the period had a pronounced effect on jewelry design. As the whole aspect of women's dress radically changed, so the type and look and placement of jewelry changed too. As women's fashions became plainer jewelry played an increasingly important role, often providing the only decorative element in a woman's dress. Long ropes of pearls or bead necklaces (of

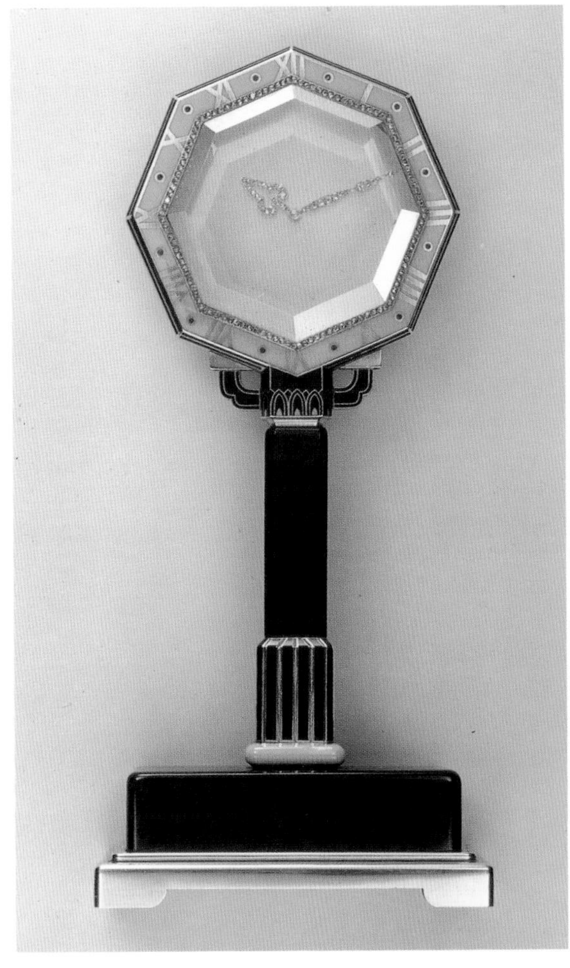

Left: Cartier's 'mystery' clock with crystal face, 1921.

Right: This ring by Jean Desprès is typical of his geometrical style.

coral, lapis lazuli, jade, agate, mother-of-pearl), *sautoirs* and pendant necklaces were worn to the waist or even to the knees to accentuate the vertical lines of the new tubular dresses. These ropes were worn in a multitude of different ways: down the back or tossed over a shoulder, knotted and looped. With their heavy tassels and pendants they were designed to sway gently to the movement of the wearer; jewels perpetually in motion. Bracelets were flat, articulated bands, often worn two or more to one arm. When the full flapper style was in fashion, arms were bared and wide bangles known as slave bracelets were worn on the upper arm, as well as quantities of smaller bracelets and bangles. The brutally short hair cuts were softened and feminized with the addition of dangling pendant earrings, worn long to emphasize the length of the neck. Jeweled bandeaux worn about the head replaced the tiara for evening wear. By day cloche hats, pulled down over the eyes, were frequently decorated with jewels, buckles and particularly the little clips that became ubiquitous in the 1930s. These little clips were also worn on shoulders, sleeves, hips, belts, in the hair for evening, and in the hollow of the back when the back decolleté became fashionable. At first they were designed as fruit baskets, stylized flower bouquets, or more abstract scrolled composition. Larger brooches were often composed of rings of carved rock crystal, jade, onyx or coral surmounted with other stones. Rings were generally large and simple, often set with single stones.

The wristwatch became popular in the early Art Deco period, a fashion that was led by the tennis star Suzanne Lenglen. These were worn with silk or leather straps by day, while the evening version was a jeweled bracelet with a tiny, almost invisible face. In the latter half of the 1920s the pendant watch came into its own,

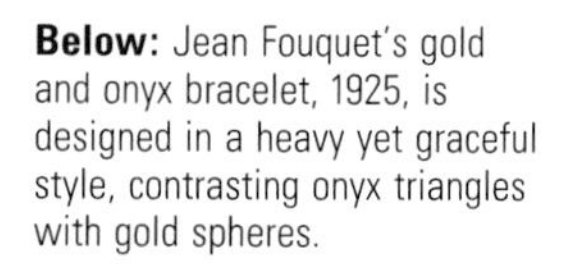

Below: Jean Fouquet's gold and onyx bracelet, 1925, is designed in a heavy yet graceful style, contrasting onyx triangles with gold spheres.

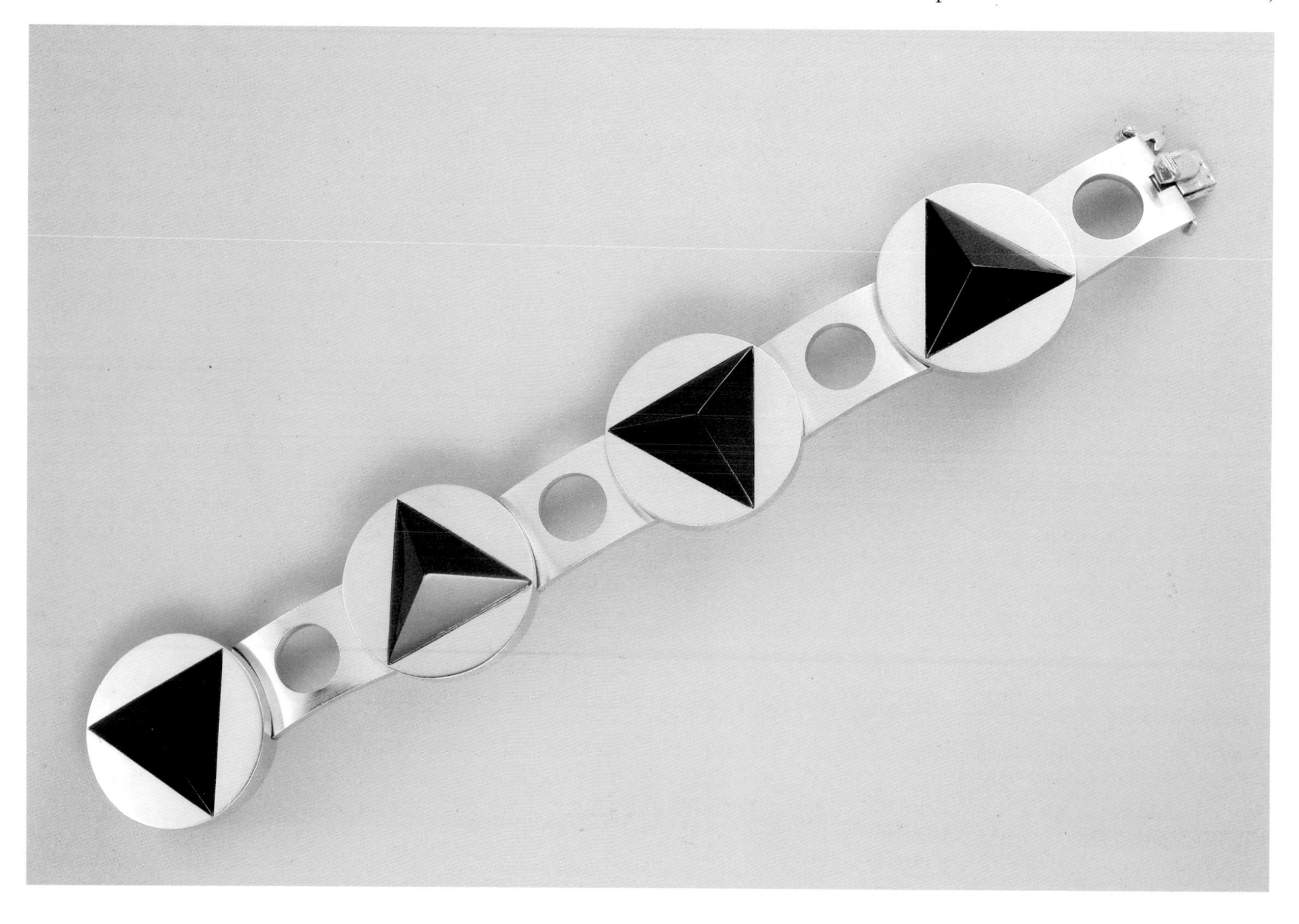

and was worn as a jewel with the watch face hidden from view. Watches and cufflinks decorated in simple colorful geometrical designs were the only jeweled objects worn by men.

Louis Cartier was responsible for guiding the Cartier firm into the new mode of design. From quite early on in his career he abandoned traditional design techniques and methods of setting jewels, and became one of the pioneering exponents of the multicolored mixing of precious and non-precious stones. He shared the prevalent Ballets Russes-inspired enthusiasm for the exotic, particularly Persian and Oriental style. Georges Fouquet worked in a less elaborate idiom, despite the fact that he had begun his career as an Art Nouveau jeweler. His designs were simple and dramatic, employing the full range of colorful hardstones.

René Lalique's jewelry design gave way to his interest in glass but he did continue to create some jewelry, mostly pendants of tinted and molded glass. These were hung on long, tasseled, silk cords or strings of glass beads, and decorated with typical motifs: insects, flowers, nymphs, leaves or animals. He also designed molded glass plaques to be set into metal frames for brooches, and flexible bracelets made of glass sections strung together on elastic cords. Other glassworkers, particularly the *pâte de verre* specialists, also designed glass jewelry.

A number of designers worked in a radical Modernist style that was clearly, if not directly, related to the stark functionalism of the Bauhaus. Gérard Sandoz, Jean Fouquet, Jean Desprès, Suzanne Belperron, Raymond Templier and Paul Brandt all contributed an abstract, machined aspect to jewelry designed in the 1920s and 1930s. In the world of high-class jewelry they formed an avant-garde, seeking to break completely with traditional ornamental styles and to create a new idiom for jewelry design, based on modern architectural and sculptural forms and inspired by the machine and the dynamics of speed. Much of their work also showed an awareness and appreciation of contemporary painting. The jumble of colors gave way to muted metallic tones highlighted with the addition of a single gem, or stark contrasts of black, red and white. Under their influence jewelry became angular and geometrical, bolder and less complex. They stressed the need for simplicity and the importance of being able to read a piece from a distance. More concerned with a high standard of design and innovative use of materials than with creating pieces of staggering expense, they began to blur the distinction between costume jewelry and *haute joaillerie*. Materials were chosen chiefly for their aesthetic and tactile qualities.

Most of this group were members of the Union des Artistes Modernes, of which Raymond Templier was a founding member. He developed a graceful modernistic style that was less harsh and aggressive than work by other artists. His simple geometrical patterns and juxtapositions of materials, particularly the varied tones of gold, platinum, and even stainless steel, were highly inventive. He often combined platinum and diamonds. Jean Fouquet, son of Georges, was a far more radical designer than his father. He too worked in a stark geometrical style, and such decoration as he used was engine-turned. He liked to contrast the tones of metals and juxtapose matt, highly polished and grooved surfaces with the contrasting textures of cut jewels or the carved hemisphere of a hardstone, usually in an assymetrical composition. His approach was sculptural and tactile, based on a play of relief against flat surfaces.

The best of Gérard Sandoz's work was confined to the latter half of the 1920s, and he gave up designing jewelry in 1931 to become a film director and painter. Even his early jewelry designs are absolutely stark and modernistic, inspired by Cubist forms and industrial parts. Metals are notched and incised, matt and polished, and generally set with a large single stone; cool metallic tones contrast with the relative warmth of labradorite, citrine or coral. Overlapping, assymetrical forms are characteristic of his style. He designed a range of lacquered cigarette cases, compacts and pocket

Above: Cartier's diamond, black onyx and emerald bangle, 1920s, with panther-head clasps.

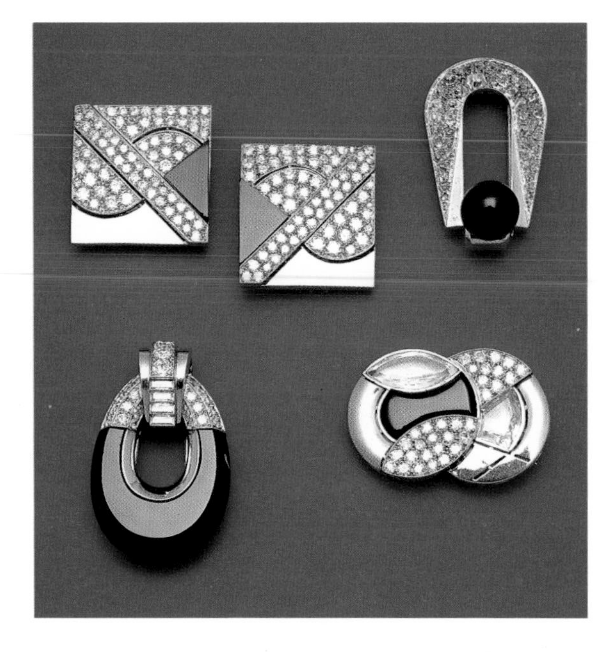

Right (clockwise from top left): Pair of clips, diamonds, onyx, white gold and platinum, c. 1925 by Paul Brandt; brooch, *pavé* diamonds, onyx and platinum, c. 1925 by Raymond Templier; brooch, rock crystal, onyx and white gold, c. 1930 by Paul Brandt; brooch, diamonds, onyx and white gold, c. 1925 by Mauboussin; all examples of the use of geometrical motifs.

Opposite: Necklace of silver, glass, imitation pearls and rhinestones, 1923, by Coco Chanel, who made costume jewelry fashionable.

Below: Chrome and bakelite necklaces, c. 1925, designed in a heavy primitive style.

Below right Mother-of-pearl, coral and diamond cigarette case, reminiscent in style of Oriental lacquerwork.

watches decorated with bold geometrical motifs in primary colors.

Jean Desprès began as early as 1912 to experiment with translating forms based on machine parts into jewelry design. He was trained as a silversmith and executed his own designs, working almost exclusively in metal, occasionally adding a little lacquer for contrast. His bracelets often have a textured hand-beaten surface. His work, made up of pure geometrical forms derived from industry, was highly sculptural, composed of spheres, cylinders and cubes.

The lacquer master and metalworker Jean Dunand designed some lacquered jewelry, as well as vanity and cigarette cases decorated with abstract geometrical patterns on a silver ground. His thick cuffs of metal inspired by African jewelry are particularly fine pieces.

Most of the jewelers of the day designed a wide range of acessories including compacts, cigarette cases, long cigarette holders that often matched bracelets and earrings, and dazzling encrusted handbags. The long lean lady simpering into her compact mirror or gesticulating with her cigarette holder is an archtypal image of the 1920s. Women flaunted their newly acquired freedom as much with their short dresses and short hair cuts as in the act of smoking or making up in public. Compacts, lipstick cases, vanity cases and cigarette cases were miniature *objets d'art* encrusted with jewels, hardstones, mother-of-pearl, shagreen or crushed eggshell, lacquer or enamel. Vanity

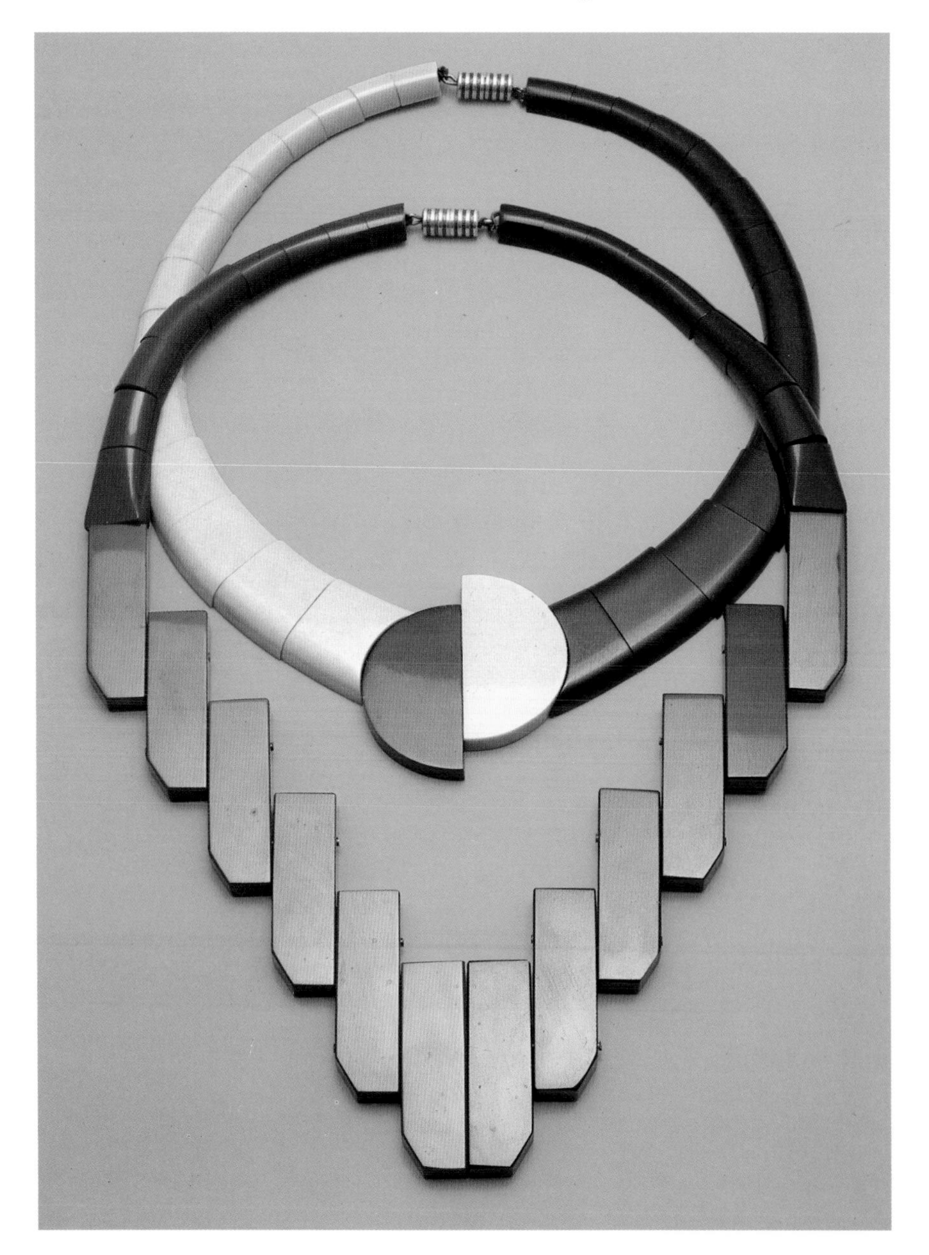

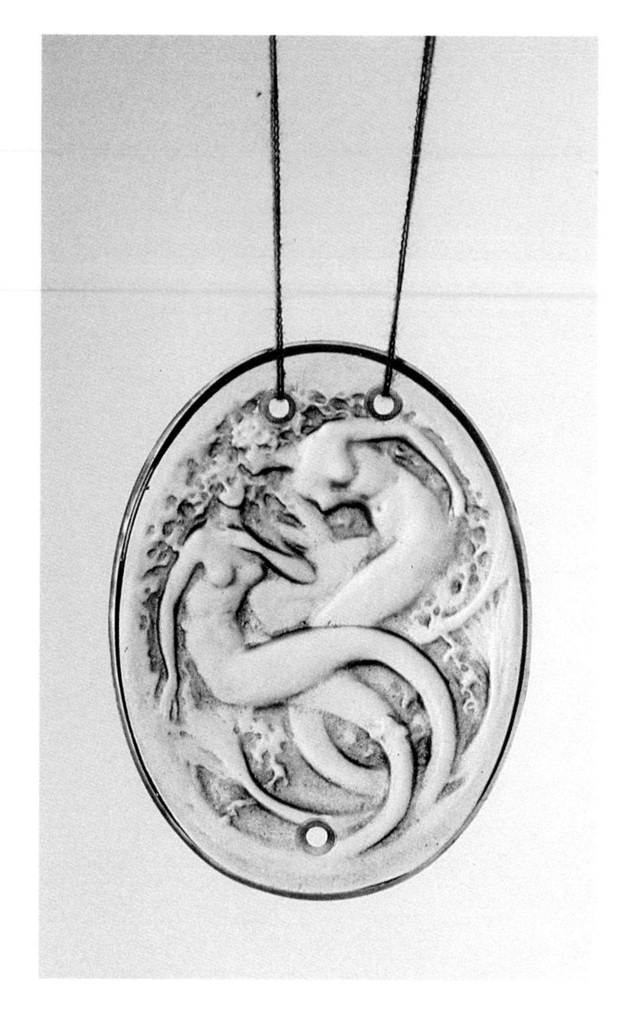

Right: René Lalique's molded glass pendant features the same fish-tailed sirens as his opalescent glass bowl (page 90).

cases depicting little Japanese, Chinese, Egyptian or Persian scenes were very popular. A *nécessaire* or vanity case contained compartments for lipstick, mirror, compact and comb, sometimes even a tiny watch face, and was often hung on a tasseled silk cord like a little handbag. A variation on this theme was the *minaudière*, devised by Alfred Van Cleef in 1930 and so named because of the way women presented themselves before its little mirror (*minauder*, in French, meaning to simper). The most precious of these vanity cases were encrusted with diamonds and precious stones. Cigarette cases were only marginally less decorative, often carved from jade, lapis or some other hardstone. Raymond Templier, Paul Brandt, Jean Dunand and Gérard Sandoz applied brightly colored geometrical motifs to their cigarette cases. Sandoz favored crushed eggshell, colored lacquers and silver. Handbags were lavish creations made of exotic fabrics, brocades and embroidered silks or animal skins, and the frames and clasps were studded with jewels. Sequined and beaded handbags were also popular. Decorative motifs were as fantastical as any that adorned the little vanity cases.

Georges Bastard designed intricate, precious, jewel-like objects and accessories; he was famous for his fans inlaid with patterns of contrasting shades of mother-of-pearl. He made jewelry in ivory, mother-of-pearl, jade and coral, and plain little boxes and bowls in materials such as ivory, rock crystal and agate.

Jeweled clocks were popular during the Deco period, and grew increasingly ingenious in their design. The jewelers strayed over into the clockmakers' territory, while interior designers and *ensembliers* had also begun to produce their own clock designs. Of all the important jewelers, Cartier was most involved with clock design and produced some exquisite little jeweled clocks, known as mystery clocks because the mechanization was so cleverly concealed. The face was transparent, made of carved quartz, rock crystal or citrine, and the frame was usually built up of a quantity of other hardstones set with colored gems. Some were elaborate jeweled fantasies on the theme of Japanese or Egyptian temples.

Below: Bracelet cuff in silver, platinum, gold, onyx and diamonds, late 1920s, by Raymond Templier. The diamond and onyx brooch is detachable and can be worn separately.

Several designers of the period were drawn to the new synthetic materials available, and the possibilities they offered of creating bright attractive jewelry that was also cheap. Even as early as 1911 Paul Iribe was designing jewelry to go with the Poiret turbans; pieces that were cheap enough to be discarded when no longer in fashion. It was Coco Chanel, however, who made costume jewelry high fashion. Her designs made no pretence to be real jewelry and were intended to be worn with tweeds, sweaters and other informal day wear. Most of the large jewelry firms produced seasonal collections of costume jewelry in response to the fashion that Chanel had launched. The profusion of cheap manufactured jewelry exhibited at the 1925 Exposition showed how far this craze had caught on, with copper, silver,

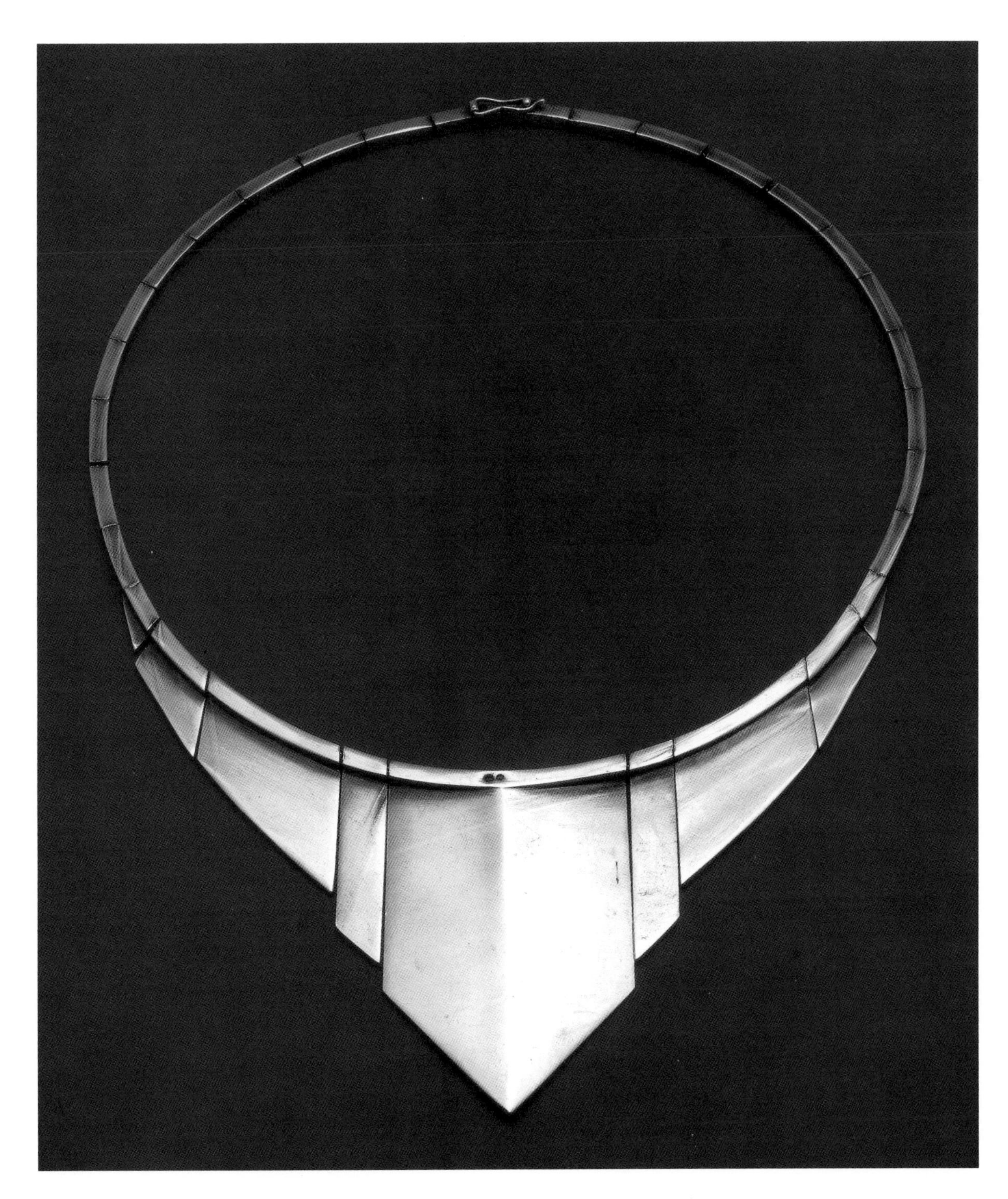

Left: Jean Desprès's silver necklace, c. 1925.

chrome, glass, fake pearls, enamel and some plastic being employed. From the mid-1920s bakelite and other synthetic resins came increasingly into use, first in mottled shades imitating marble, tortoiseshell, horn and amber, then in juxtapositions of bright colors. Other materials used were paste, base metal, and marcasite (little studs of cut steel). Cheap compacts and vanity cases were produced in vast quantities in chrome and enamel and decorated with bright jazzy designs in geometrical and zigzag patterns. It was French costume jewelry, more than anything else, that influenced jewelry design in other countries.

British jewelry of the 1920s was still dominated by the Arts and Crafts style, but by the 1930s cheap and cheerful designs had also become a feature of British production. Fashionable ladies bought their jewelry where they bought their dresses and hats – in Paris, although many considered the bold Parisian designs to be too showy.

After the Wall Street crash of 1929, many jewelry firms were forced to close or to reduce staff to a minimum. Costume jewelry really came into its own then, and the stock Art Deco designs were reworked in plastic and brilliants. Multiple-use jewelry was one solution – brooches that became pendants, necklaces that became bracelets. Heavy bangles and African mask brooches carved in ebony and ivory became popular, and Mauboussin and Van Cleef and Arpels designed collections inspired by African carvings. Eventually the popularity of the Art Deco style began to fade; gold replaced platinum and angularity gave way to curves.

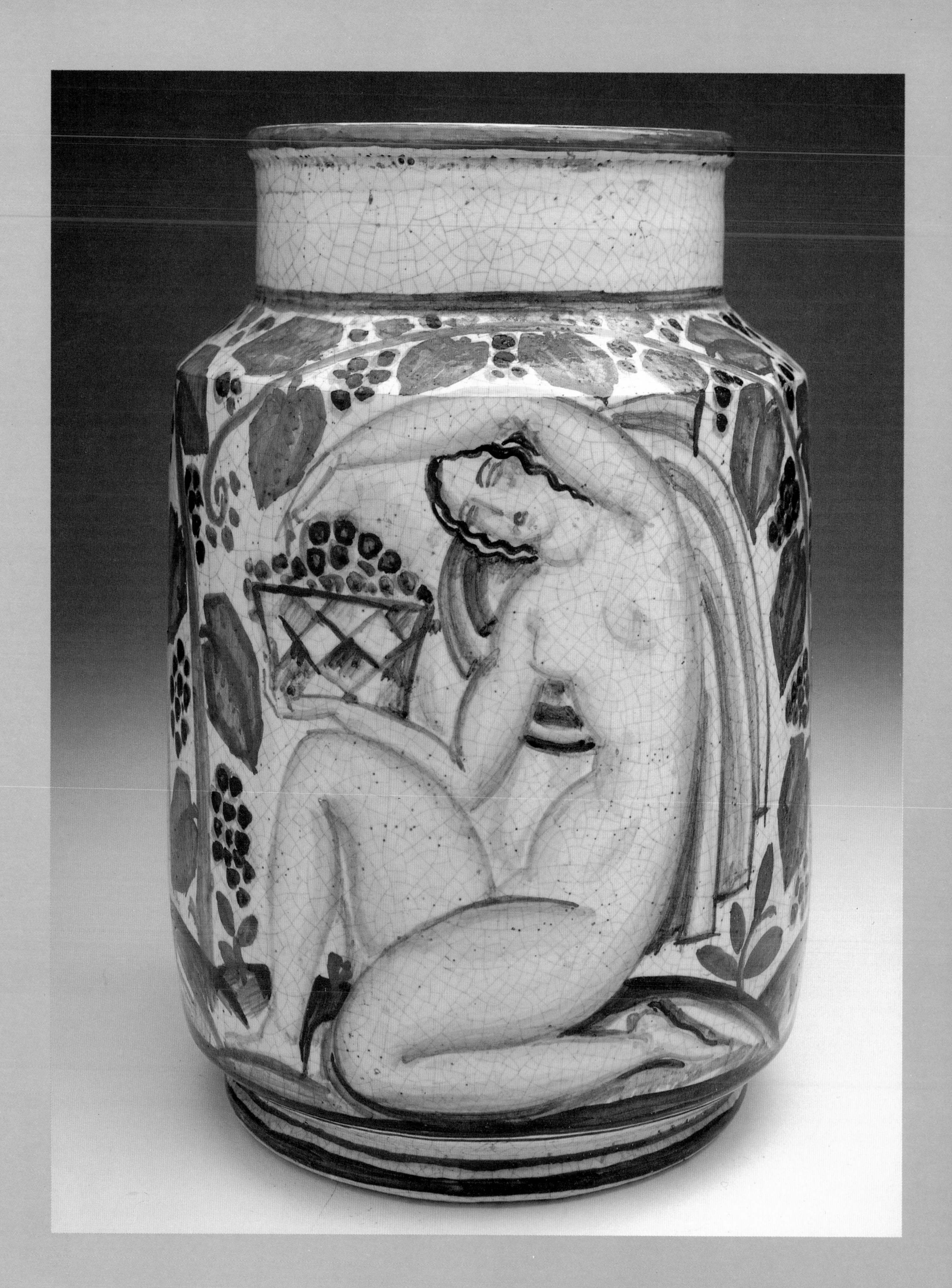

9
CERAMICS

Opposite: René Buthaud's stoneware vase features a nude similar in style to those on Lindstrand's vase for Orrefors (page 88).

Like the glassware of the period, Art Deco ceramics of good design and quality were produced in countries all over Europe. Styles were not necessarily dictated by the nucleus of French artists, although here as in other disciplines the French creative output was prodigious and influential. In fact styles were numerous and diverse, from the assertively hand-made creations of the studio potters through traditional manufacture to mass-produced tableware.

While manufacturers in the 1920s were beginning to turn out slick modern ware patterned with light Deco motifs, the studio potters, as if to assert the unique, hand-worked quality of their pieces, concentrated increasingly on craft traditions and obtaining a thorough knowledge of materials and processes of production. The period is marked by a return to the origins of the craft, and a renewed interest in the pottery of Persia and the Middle East, the Orient, Ancient Egypt and Rome.

A revival of interest in ceramics began in the late nineteenth century, and was stimulated by the prevailing fascination with Oriental art. A number of painters, sculptors and craftsmen became involved in designing ceramics and renewing links with the traditions of the craft. This interest in the arts of the East continued to influence the production of ceramics in the early part of the twentieth century. A complete mastery of technique, and particularly Oriental techniques of glazing, became of critical importance to Art Deco ceramicists.

André Metthey played a key role in the development of a new aesthetic in the pottery of the period. He created a style that was based on traditional Middle Eastern designs, with an emphasis on rich colors such as turquoises, greens and pinks, a style that effected the transition between Art Nouveau and early Deco pottery. His study of Persian and Islamic pottery led him to switch from stoneware to faïence, with its greater potential for color effects. His designs were figurative and layed out frieze-like in bands or medallions. Most of his work predates World War I and many of the motifs that he introduced became standard to Art Deco. He also invited artists such as Derain, Matisse, Bonnard and Renoir to decorate his ware.

Another important pioneer was Auguste Delaherche, who worked in stoneware and porcelain and built up a considerable store of knowledge through his research and experiments, providing an excellent base for those who came after him. From as early as 1904 he began to incline towards simpler shapes and textured surfaces. He introduced the use of ceramic panels in architecture, which became popular in the 1920s.

Jean Mayodon worked in faïence and developed a style that was notable for its thick, crackled, polychrome glazes. Like Metthey he was most interested in color and spent his career experimenting to obtain a wider variety of rich colors. He frequently applied gold luster as a highlight, a technique gleaned from a study of Islamic ceramics. His decorative themes were drawn from classical mythology – stylized animals were particular favorites – and surfaces were crackled and textured to resemble antique pottery. Hand-painted and modeled figures and animals in faïence also feature in his work. In addition to small decorative objects he executed largescale ceramic panels and tiles, many of them commissioned for the great ocean liners.

From the 1910s through to the end of the 1920s, Emile Lenoble and Emile Decoeur reigned jointly in the field of ceramic design. Korean and Chinese Sung dynasty pottery were the primary influences on Emile Lenoble's hand-turned stoneware. By mixing his clay with kaolin he achieved a remarkably delicate and lightweight stoneware. His work is characterized by its simple floral, scroll and geometrical motifs, applied in bands to set off the beautiful shapes of his vessels. These were painted beneath the glaze, incised into the slip or else carved directly onto the vessel. His colors were rich and earthy; greens, reds and browns with creamy matt glazes.

Emile Decoeur's early career was spent experimenting with stoneware and porcelain

Below: André Metthey's pottery charger, c. 1920, reflects his Orientalizing style.

Opposite below: Jean Luce's white porcelain plates painted in silver and gold combine geometrical and semi-naturalistic motifs.

techniques, from drip-glazing to enameling or painted decoration. His early pieces are decorated in a floral style similar to Lenoble's work, applied in light relief to enhance the shapes. But his concern with harmonizing shape, color and the surface treatment of his wares led him to abandon conventional decoration altogether. His mature work dates from the early 1920s; forms are simple and elegant and clad in heavy, luscious, monochromatic glazes, while decoration is restricted to a little incised banding or a dark outline around the rim of a vessel.

The work of Lenoble and Decoeur shows clearly that the prevailing tendency was to simplify decorative effects and focus instead on texture, color and form. George Serré's thick stoneware vases, rough-textured and incised with chevrons and other geometrical patterns, are a good example of the move toward texture and simplicity of form.

Ceramicists of the period were fascinated with glaze techniques, and there was much experimentation with new glazes and revival of old ones. Edmond Lachenal was notable for having developed a kind of *flambé* glaze resembling cloisonné enamel, which he applied decoratively over a pale crackled ground.

The Fleming Henri Simmen was influenced by Oriental ceramics and traveled extensively in the Far East, studying the ancient traditions and techniques of the craft. As a result of his research he was able to devise a method of working using only organic ingredients and modeling by hand, rather than turning at the wheel. The shapes of his vessels were based on organic forms, and any chemical impurities in the material were manipulated for decorative effect. Occasionally he carved abstract motifs in light relief to enhance his glazes, which were thick and crackled. Colors included a brilliant turquoise blue, often on a cracked ivory or beige ground. He made salt-glaze, with its attractive speckled effect, a speciality. His

Above: Incised and enameled sandstone vase, c. 1912, by Emile Lenoble.

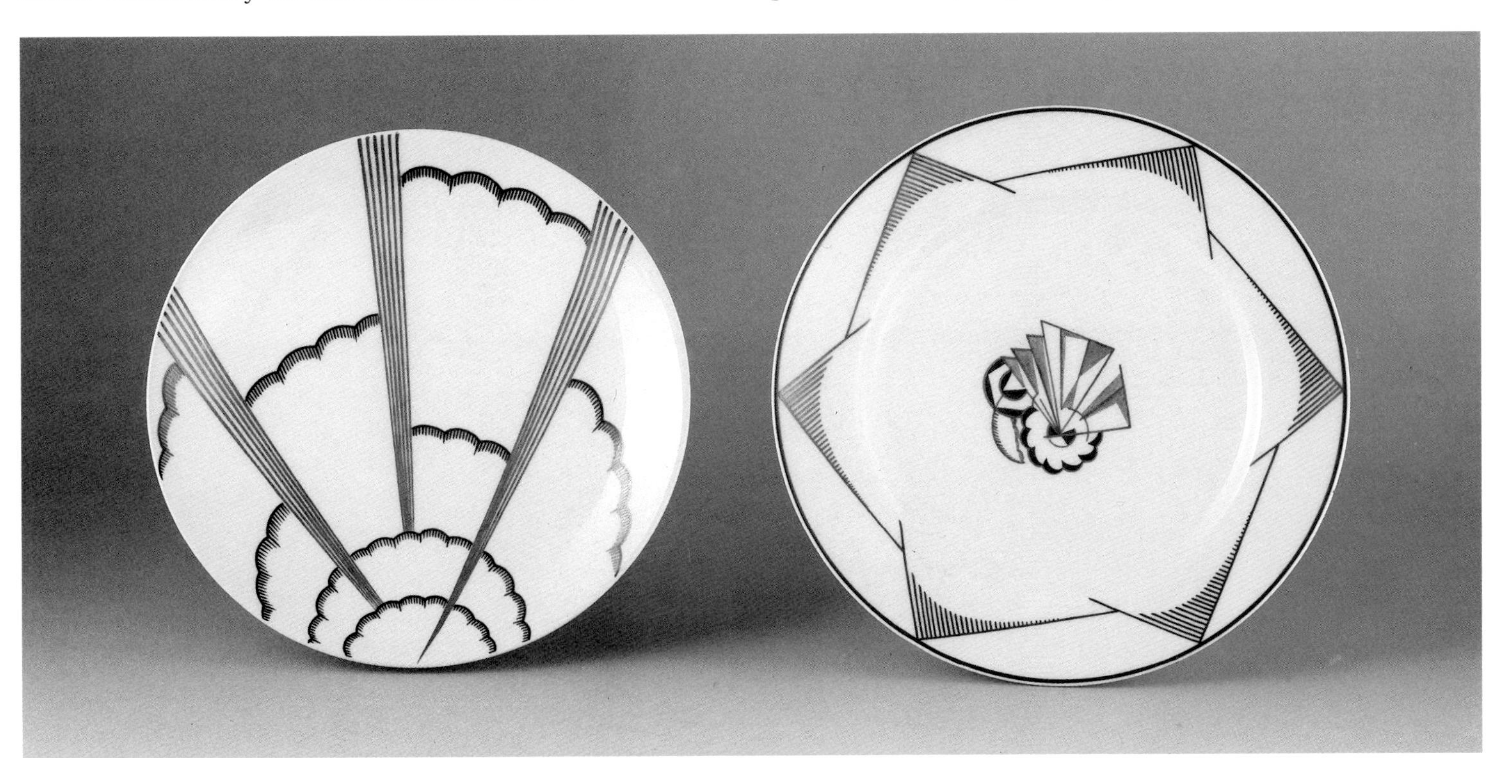

Right: The flower motif on Emile Decoeur's turned and glazed stoneware vase, c. 1910, recalls Oriental lacquerware.

Far right: This enameled sandstone vase, c. 1925, by Emile Decoeur is more restrained in both shape and decoration.

Below right: Jean Mayodon's platter in glazed polychrome stoneware with gold strands, c. 1925.

Japanese wife, Mme O'Kin Simmen, carved delicate stoppers, lids and handles in ivory, horn and precious woods to decorate his pieces.

Earthenware was less popular in this period than stoneware and porcelain, but a few artists preferred its smooth glazed surface as a ground for their painterly decorations. René Buthaud was one of a number of talented artists from Bordeaux who worked in the Art Deco style. His fascination with African tribal art is reflected both in the forms and in the decorative themes of his work. His earthenware vases are large and bulbous, often resembling gourds and frequently painted with exotic black women against a background of tropical fronds and stylized animals. He worked in an expressive linear style, outlining his figures in black or brown and then frequently applying washes of color,

Right: Vally Wieselthier's glazed pottery candleholder, executed at the Wiener Werkstätte, c. 1924, is characteristic of her robust figural style.

Opposite: Carter, Stabler and Adams's colorful earthenware pot, 1920s, features both floral and geometrical motifs.

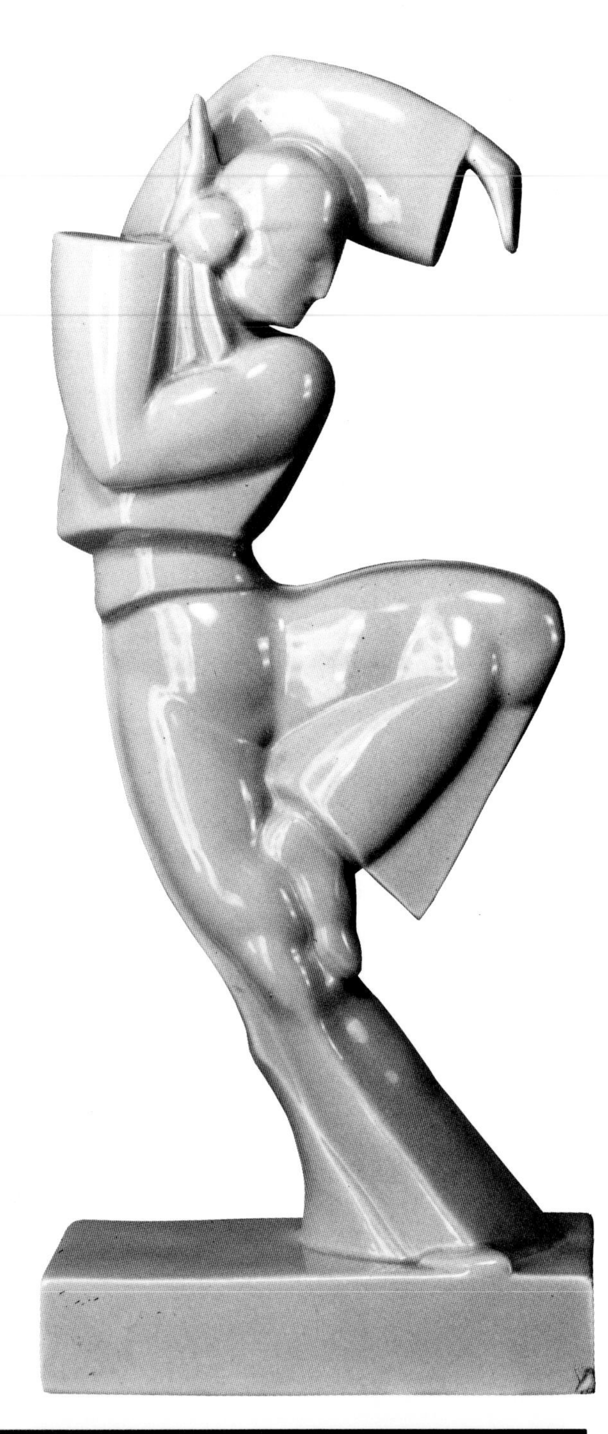

Right: Porcelain dancing figure, c. 1930, by the Parisian retailer Robj.

Below: Porcelain teapot decorated in the Russian Suprematist style, after a design by Chasnik.

usually over a crackled glaze. From 1913 until 1926 he held the post of artistic director of the Primavera ceramics factory. Francis Jourdain designed earthenware and varnished clay dinner services that were simple and robust-looking with minimal decoration, which he sold from his own shop.

In ceramics, as in other areas of design, the Wiener Werkstätte style lost some of its early severity. In the 1920s Susi Singer and Vally Wieselthier created roughly modeled pottery figures in lively drip-glazed colors, while Josef Hoffman and Michael Powolny designed simple and elegant modern tableware.

British studio pottery became important at this time, chiefly due to the talents of Bernard Leach, who studied in Japan and in 1920 set up a pottery in St Ives, Cornwall, with a young Japanese potter named Hamada Shoji. His work and teaching focused on folk traditions in pottery, and his special interest was in slipware. A number of his pupils became prominent potters in their own right, all working after his manner in earthy colors and undecorated slip. Katherine Pleydell-Bouverie, for example, developed a style of extreme simplicity and concentrated on perfecting a type of glaze made from wood ash.

Carter, Stabler and Adams were based in Poole, Dorset, and produced sophisticated handmade pottery for domestic and architectural use. This was decorated with floral designs in soft colors which display the influence of the Werkstätte potters.

Little porcelain figurines were popular during this period; a cheap alternative to chryselephantine and bronze statuary, they were often intended to be collected in series. They were generally highly stylized and included lively, colorful and often humorous caricatures of stars of the screen, stage and music halls, jazz singers and musicians. The Parisian retailers Robj sold figurines and decanters designed by a number of artists in addition to their other wares. The sculptors Joël and Jan Martel were well known for their series of animal sculptures in ceramic. Wiener Werkstätte artists Susi Singer and Vally Wieselthier worked in a figural style and splashed their appealing, roughly modeled pieces with vibrantly colored glazes. Clarice Cliff created original variations on the figurine theme. She designed two-dimensional cut-out shapes painted with lively dashes and spots of color to suggest the outlines of her figures. The Royal Dux company, originally of Bohemia (now part of Czechoslovakia) produced vividly glazed figurines in an exotic high Deco style.

The new creative fervor affected the ceramics industry as much as it did studio ceramics and, after a long decline in standards and endless degraded copies of past styles, the period saw the beginnings of a thorough moderniza-

Left: Porcelain tea service, late 1920s, by Edouard-Marcel Sandoz for Théodore Haviland.

tion of serial production tableware. The influence of the Bauhaus was enormous; though its specific contribution to ceramics was small, the strength of its ideals, and their successful application to other areas of design, helped to spread its influence, with most immediate effect on the ceramics industry within Germany. The Staatliche-Porzellan Fabrik in Berlin took on an ex-Bauhaus pupil, Marguerite Friedlander-Wildenhain, as designer. Her functional wares were virtually undecorated except for a little banding, while Trude Petri's 'Urbino' service of 1930 for the Arzberg Porcelain Works was absolutely plain.

An important influence on European ceramics was Soviet Constructivist porcelain, which was exhibited and much admired at the 1925 Exposition. Its dynamic modern style had much in common with Art Deco, but its propagandist and political content set it in quite another category.

In the nineteenth century a rift had occurred between the pottery industries and the individual potters and this separation still existed in the Deco period, particularly in France and Germany. The Arts and Crafts movement had done much to cause this rift, because the artist-potter, while gaining status, disdained industrial collaboration.

In the French ceramics industry the development of a modern style was slow and there were many misguided attempts to adapt to Art Deco. The Sèvres company, for example, made efforts to modernize its style but the results were often poor. One of its mistakes was to commission designs from well-known artists who had no experience of ceramic design, though designs by Ruhlmann, Lalique, Dufy and the Martel brothers were more successful than most.

In general forms remained conventional or else, in a vain attempt to be modern, became aggressively angular. Decorative motifs more quickly reflected the prevailing fashions – although these were often insensitively applied. Theodore Haviland et Cie of Limoges

Below: Boldly geometrical tea service by Primavera, 1920s.

APOLLONIA
EMERENZIANA
AGATA

Opposite: This porcelain vase by Gio Ponti for Richard Ginori features a complicated three-dimensional effect of nudes and classical architecture.

Left: The classical simplicity of Jean Luce's teapot and sucrier, late 1920s, is relieved only by the scrolled handles.

was one of the companies which contributed a stylish and modernistic range of wares. Among the designers who worked for them were Edouard Sandoz, who created charming animal figures in porcelain, and Suzanne Lalique, daughter of the great *maître verrier*. Jean Luce designed stylish ceramic tableware and glassware, and was careful to modernize both form and decoration. The simplicity of his work reflects the prevailing tendency; his tableware, in particular, was cleverly co-ordi-

Left: Vegetable dish, 1930s, by Susie Cooper.

Below: This assortment of pottery pitchers and vases, c. 1930, by Clarice Cliff shows her use of juxtaposed bright colors.

Above: Stoneware and pottery vases, c. 1925, by Charles Catteau.

Below: The severe style of Keith Murray's vase for Wedgwood is in strong contrast to the work of Catteau.

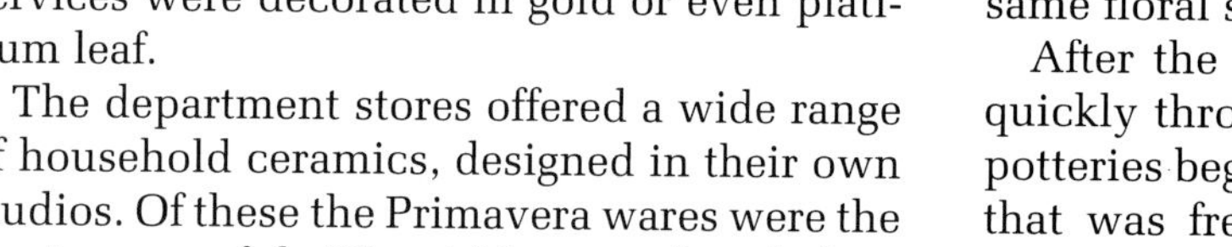

nated with a scattering of geometrical motifs, either painted by hand or from stencils. Luxury services were decorated in gold or even platinum leaf.

The department stores offered a wide range of household ceramics, designed in their own studios. Of these the Primavera wares were the most successful. Süe et Mare produced their

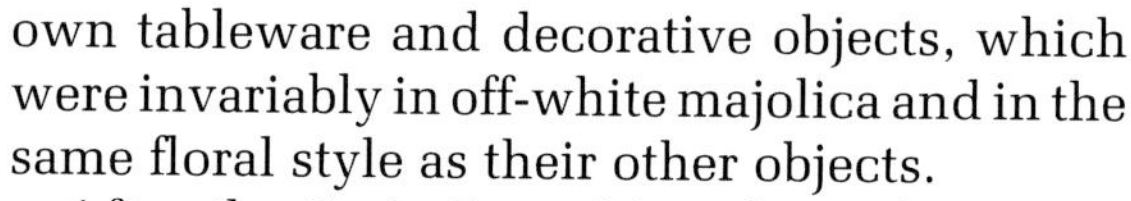

own tableware and decorative objects, which were invariably in off-white majolica and in the same floral style as their other objects.

After the Paris Exposition the style spread quickly through Europe, and many industrial potteries began to offer wares in a diluted style that was frequently insensitive, eccentric or even vulgar. A number of Belgian firms were more successful than French manufacturers in creating a Deco idiom suitable for mass-produced ceramics. The best Art Deco wares were produced by the Keramis factory, owned by Boch *frères*, whose most notable designer was the Frenchman Charles Catteau. Parisian high Deco motifs, especially the angularized rose, decorate his stoneware and glazed faïence in cloisonné patterns, often on a thick white craquelure or crazed ground.

The best Italian contribution to Art Deco ceramics was made by Gio Ponti, a versatile artist who worked in many disciplines. He designed ceramics for the factory of the Società Ceramica Richard-Ginori in an idiosyncratic style that was partly neoclassical in inspiration. His work acknowledged contemporary tendencies but was not dependent on them. Many of his ceramics are adorned with mannered female nudes reclining against architectural backgrounds.

Several factories in Denmark produced art pottery, in the contemporary style, including Bing and Grøndahl. They mastered a wide range of different techniques and had a number

Left: 'Argenta' ceramic vase, 1930s, by Wilhelm Kåge for Gustavsberg.

of talented artists working for them, including Jean Gauguin, son of the painter, who sculpted in glazed faïence.

In Britain Susie Cooper and Clarice Cliff are the best known of those who designed Deco ceramics. Clarice Cliff brightened British tables with her highly original and colorful designs, the colors inspired by the Ballet Russes; strident combinations of bright purple and orange (the famous Art Deco orange known as 'tango') were her particular favorites. She began her career at the age of 16 as a transfer print designer for A J Wilkinson Ltd and in 1939 became artistic director of the company and the related Newport Pottery Company. Her wares, designed in series with names like 'Bizarre', 'Biarritz', and 'Fantasque', were relatively cheap and immensely popular. Her designs are bold and crudely painted; bright geometrical themes as well as fruit, flowers and fantasy landscapes decorate forms that are often somewhat angularized.

Susie Cooper, on the other hand, introduced a quieter note of Modernism into her designs. She was greatly influenced by French Deco and is said to have radically changed her style as a result of her visit to the 1925 Exposition. She spent her early career decorating blanks for Gray's pottery and set up her own company in 1929. Her work was elegant, and decorated with stylized patterns or simple bands of muted color. The New Zealand architect Keith Murray represented an even more starkly Modernist approach to design with his minimalist machine-age pieces made for Josiah Wedgwood and Sons. His classic forms were clad in monochromatic glazes in cool colors decorated only with a few engine-turned incisions or parallel grooves.

Cubism had a pronounced effect on Czech decorative arts in the 1910s and this was apparent in some of the ceramic pieces produced, with their strange angular shapes and stark geometrical decorations, while more traditional potteries turned out designs equivalent to the Parisian high Deco.

Much of the Scandinavian ceramic output of this period displays a functionalist aesthetic, and in general artists were involved with industrial design. The work of the Swede Wilhelm Kåge is particularly notable. He was Artistic Director of the Gustavsberg Porcelain Works and designed tableware specifically for those with low incomes, as well as a series of stoneware pieces chased in silver with single stylized motifs on a greeny-glaze background – vases, bowls, plates and boxes – which he titled 'Argenta'. His simple faïence tableware drew on traditional design, but was at the same time functional and modern.

In the 1930s the professional industrial designer emerged to bridge the gap between art and industry, and was responsible for the design of simple unadorned mass-produced tableware, designs which were also adopted by plastics manufacturers.

Below: Wilhelm Kåge's 'Argenta' pot with classical figure applied in silver, 1930s, for Gustavsberg.

VOGUE

Modes d'Automne, Chapeaux et Tissus Nouveaux

Revue Mensuelle

10
FASHION

Opposite: Georges Lepape's *Vogue* cover, Autumn 1927, is in his characteristically mannered style.

A study of Art Deco would not be complete without mention of the revolutionary changes in women's fashion that took place in the first decades of the twentieth century. These changes reflect the profound alterations in the economic and social structure that were equally a factor in the evolution of the decorative arts.

In this period fashion and interior design developed almost in unison away from past styles, absorbing influences from literature, the theatre, ballet and the fine arts. Couturiers, designers and craftsmen all drew on the same sources of inspiration in their quest for modernity, and Oriental, Persian, and Egyptian art, even Cubism, were plundered for new styles and motifs.

Jacques Doucet and Paul Poiret, the great personalities of the fashion world, were instrumental in developing the Art Deco style and introducing new sources of design. Doucet was most important as a patron, imposing his taste to some degree on the artists whose work he commissioned, and helping to develop a strain of Art Deco that was less dependent on traditional sources and more in tune with developments in the fine arts. By setting himself up both as couturier and interior designer, Poiret imposed an even greater unity on dress and decor. To a lesser degree fashion designers such as Madeleine Vionnet, Jeanne Lanvin and Suzanne Talbot helped to endorse this alliance, by patronizing the most fashionable designers and by allowing their interiors to be publicized in the interior decorating magazines.

The Art Deco interior as setting or backdrop for fashion plates or photographs made frequent appearance in contemporary fashion albums. Poiret set the example by posing his creations among piles of plump cushions. Later fashion plates frequently depicted ladies gathering for cocktails in an immaculate modern interior fitted out with the latest Art Deco accessories. To advertise a new perfume, Suzanne Talbot had herself photographed reclining on her *pirogue* sofa against the lacquered walls that Eileen Gray had designed for her. Leitmotifs of the Deco interior such as the stylized rose, the exotic bird or the greyhound featured in the fashion plates, while Oriental or tropical scenes often served as backdrops.

The changes in women's fashions were bound up with the changing role of women in society. The importance of the revolution that took place can only be fully appreciated by returning to the beginning of the century and tracing developments from there. Nothing could have been more different from the over-elaborate and constricting fashions of the turn of the century than the styles that were beginning to predominate 20 or so years later. In the early years of the century fashion was the exclusive domain of the wealthy – a display of utter extravagance. A lady of the upper classes was expected to make the business of dress her *raison d'être*, for fashion etiquette was highly elaborate and there were numerous changes of toilette to be made in a day. A mature, womanly figure was fashionable; women compressed themselves into tight-laced corsets

Right: Norma Talmadge in *The Woman Disputed* directed by Henry King, 1928. The floppy brimmed hat, dangling earrings, strings of beads and long feather boa were typical accessories of the 1920s. Note too the heavily outlined eyes and cupid-bow mouth.

Opposite: Coco Chanel in a jersey suit and sweater of her own design, and wearing the multiple strands of pearls that she made popular, 1929.

that reduced the waist to tiny proportions and arched the back so that the bust was thrown forward. All manner of cumbersome petticoats and undergarments were worn. Blouses and dresses frothed with lace and other trimmings. Hair was puffed and padded and crowned by gigantic, over-decorated hats which were secured with long pins. Women were strait-jacketed by their clothes which made it impossible for them to move freely and forced them into dependence on their servants and their menfolk. These restrictions reflected the more general social restrictions that women had to endure.

Since the 1880s women had been taking part increasingly in various sports, and here their elaborate clothes had become more and more of a handicap. A lady might risk her reputation if she were seen in bloomers riding a bicycle around the turn of the century. Even the female tennis stars were cautious of altering their costumes in ways which might be considered too radical, and until the 1920s they played in long skirts, stockings and hats. Around 1910 the bathing suit was introduced, which was less ridiculous than the Edwardian dresses worn with bloomers but was still long and voluminous.

The new dances, including the famous Tango and Charleston, that were imported from America necessitated greater freedom of movement; only the latest Poiret gown with side vents could cope with such frenzied activity. The new dances and the fashions that they gave rise to were endlessly inveighed against, but to little avail. Even before World War I nightclubs were springing up in most European towns, and the craze for these dances was to increase throughout the 1920s.

Poiret worked for a time at the Maison Doucet before taking a position at the House of Worth. There he was given the job of catering for the large numbers of society ladies who demanded that simple and practical dresses be made for them. This project proved too innovative for the Worth establishment and Poiret was asked to leave after only a short time, but he had learned a valuable lesson regarding women's attitude to dress. It is important to stress the role played by women themselves in effecting change, for they began increasingly to rebel against the expensive, time-consuming and unaccommodating fashions. Sensing that the way forward in fashion was to continue to simplify and straighten lines, Poiret set up on his own in 1904. His tailored costume, adapted from the motoring suit, was enthusiastically taken up; it was chic but, most important, it was comfortable and allowed greater ease of movement. Poiret claimed to have liberated women from the tight-laced corset by reintroducing the Empire-line dress. Although he did not banish

Above: Dresses by Paul Poiret from the *Gazette du Bon Ton*, 1914; the angular style of illustration complements the straight lines of the dresses.

Below: This illustration of a Poiret gown of 1911 by Georges Lepape shows Poiret's typical scatter of plump cushions.

the corset altogether, he certainly rid fashion of the distorting s-shaped corset and reverted to a line that followed more or less the natural contours of the body. Stomach and waist were eased out of their former constrictions and dresses hung straight from just beneath the bust. He devised a quantity of dresses in the Empire style, with ample sleeves and low necklines. He simplified styles, abolishing excessive ornamentation and concentrating on line, color and fabric.

By 1908 Poiret's style had begun to exercise a considerable influence on the development of fashion. His use of rich and exotic colors was partly stimulated by the extravagant, vibrant sets and costumes of the Ballets Russes. His early designs also correspond to the evolving Art Deco style in interiors, with its confusion of Oriental, folk and Persian influences, bright colors and patterns. Oriental costume was a great source of inspiration to him, and he adapted the kimono sleeve to his models, as well as introducing gowns that were wrapped, draped and tied with sashes, or coats that billowed out behind in the Japanese fashion. He dressed women in rich, woven silks and brocades, often in strident color combinations – in part a reaction against the delicate, pastel tones that were popular during the Edwardian era. He introduced exotic turbans and bandeaux embellished with jewels, plumes and aigrettes.

In keeping with styles of dress and interior so evocative of the East, as well as the sense of theater imparted by the Ballets Russes, make-up came increasingly into use and the fashionable face became bolder and more provocative, with heavily shaded eyes and perfect, cupid-bow mouth painted in deep red. Poiret's fashion plates of the 1910s depict graceful, stylized, dark-eyed females, tall and slender in the new straight styles.

Poiret was also responsible for the introduction of the color fashion album, in which his designs were illustrated by artists such as Georges Lepape, George Barbier and Paul Iribe. The concept was quite novel, and proved valuable publicity. Many of these plates incorporate little narratives, and depict modishly dressed women in early Art Deco interiors. The languishing pose introduced in these early plates became an enduring feature of Art Deco fashion illustration of the 1920s; decor and dress shared the same stylized gracefulness.

Just before the outbreak of World War I, further changes were made in women's dress styles. The long, tubular line was broken with a tunic that hung to the knees and in England, and to some extent in France, a long belted jumper of knitted material became popular. When war was declared in 1914, the initial assumption was that it would be a trifling affair of short duration, but it soon became clear it would be nothing of the sort. Women were needed to replace the men who had gone to the front, and they set to work in hospitals, factories, workshops and offices, adopting a style of clothing that afforded maximum comfort and practicality. Because of this need for practical clothing, as well as the need to conserve fabric for uniforms, women's clothes became very simple and standardized. Some women wore trousers at work for convenience, others simply raised the hems of their skirts, and a few even cropped their hair.

When the war was over the contribution of women to the war effort was recognized and earned them a new respect and greater independence. Among other things, they were reluctant to give up the more casual styles of dress they had adopted, and felt they had earned the right to introduce similar but more stylish innovations into fashion. Although fashion reverted to some extent to its pre-war phase, the sartorial freedom women had tasted could not be forgotten and styles now evolved faster in a search for the same degree of comfort and practicality. Nevertheless, no single dominant style emerged for some time.

It is significant that the leading couture houses that emerged after the war were run by women; Coco Chanel, Jeanne Lanvin and Madeleine Vionnet. The innovations they introduced were largely based on adaptations of men's clothing, and the ground broken temporarily during the war was now broken for good; hems came up, hair was regularly cropped, a few women began to wear trousers. The war had created a shortage of labor and more women than ever before were compelled to work, including rising numbers of middle-class women, war widows and those who had been impoverished by the war. They demanded simple, functional clothes with style and smartness, while the ever-increasing enthusiasm for sports and motoring generated more casual and liberating fashions. The young generation rebelled against convention, associating the carnage of the war with the stuffy and restricting society that had preceded it. A cult of youth developed, reflected in the fashion for the lithe, adolescent figure and a dynamic, sporting style of dress. Emphasis shifted from breast and hips to the limbs; shapeless, tubular shifts displayed to advantage long slim legs and arms.

Born of peasant stock, Coco Chanel had raised herself socially and professionally through determination and talent and was every bit a woman of the new age. From the start of her career as a designer she set about simplifying and paring down shapes, easing lines, creating a smart feminine fashion that

Above: Tunic tied with a sash worn over a draped skirt with dipped hem, illustration by George Barbier from the *Gazette du Bon Ton*, 1913.

Right: Sonia Delaunay's fashion drawings of 1922-23 show her preoccupation with simple shapes and bold geometrical patterns.

Opposite: Summer fashions in evening wear, Paris 1933, with the typical soft draping, slim cut and plunge back.

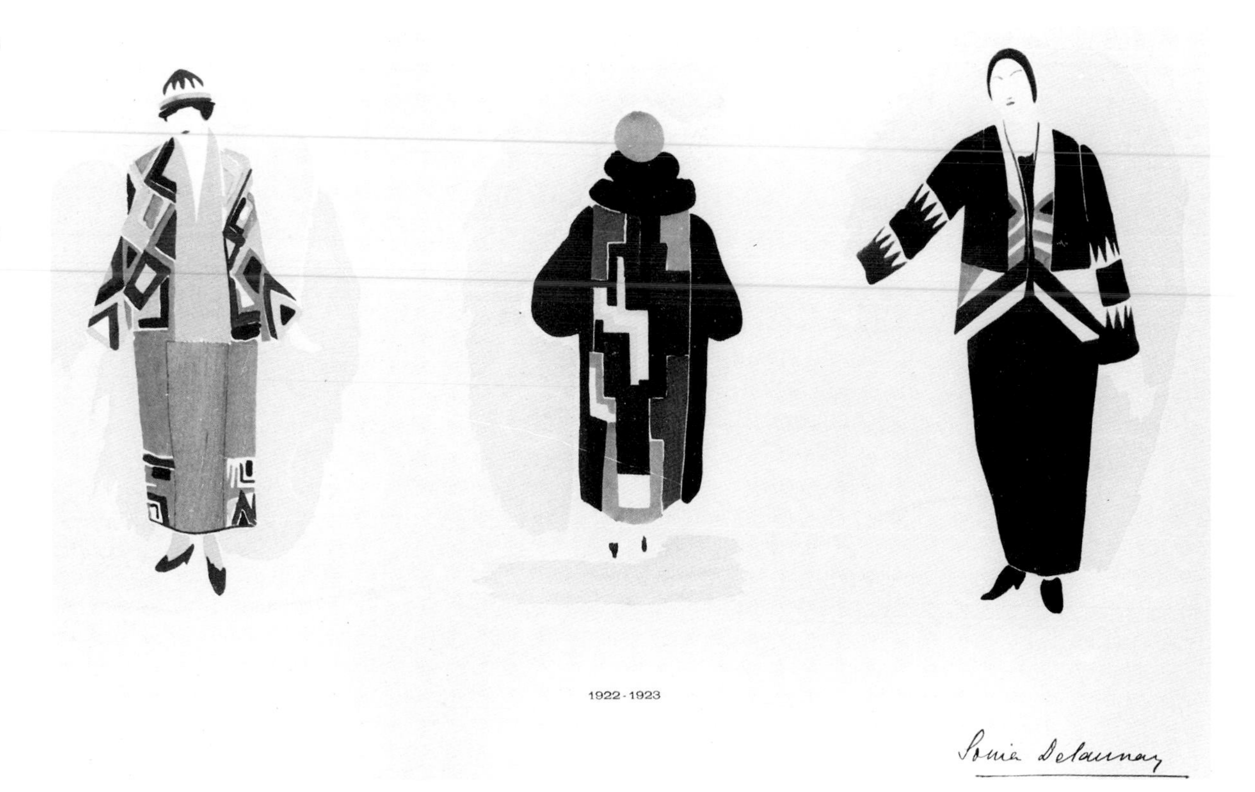

Below: Fashion of 1930 as worn by film star Norah Baring: silk chemise dress, neat cloche hat and fox stole.

was easy to wear, with elements borrowed from men's clothing and especially from casual, sporting styles. She loved tweeds and jersey fabrics and made muted earthy colors, and above all black, fashionable. She was instrumental in creating the sharper and neater 1920s style, designing jersey tunics, smart tailor-made suits, long waistless chemise dresses, long straight evening gowns which were often beaded, jersey wool dresses, and suits with simple cardigan jackets. Like the best designers working in the decorative arts, she exercised a rigorous discipline in her designs, simplifying and purifying forms, concentrating on cut and materials, controling ornament and using it to accentuate the strength of her design.

Sonia Delaunay designed fabrics for clothing as well as for decorating and upholstery, the majority of them patterned with bold geometrics in strong colors. While other couturiers took up the idea of reproducing the geometrical motifs of contemporary painting and design on cloth in a more tentative manner, Delaunay's fabrics seem fresh and dynamic even today. She sought to apply pattern in a way that would enhance the cut and rhythm of the garment when worn. Her designs for dresses were produced exclusively by the couturier Jacques Heim.

The flapper style, so often regarded as characteristic of the 1920s, did not develop overnight and was mostly confined to the period from 1925 to 1929. Skirts were not consistently short, nor dresses consistently waistless through the decade. In the early years hemlines went up and down, waists appeared and

DAVID
MODELS—GERMAINE BAILLY

disappeared, skirts were alternately flared and straight. The bobbed hairstyle sported by Irene Castle and Isadora Duncan before the war began to become popular and in the late 1920s hair was cropped even closer to the head with the introduction of the shingle. By the mid-decade the new dress silhouette had taken over: very neat, sleek and tubular, and ending just below the knee. At the height of its chic the garçonne look consisted of cropped hair, close-fitting cloche hat to emphasize the small, neat head and a long, waistless, tubular dress. Many women felt compelled to flatten their curves with corsets that thickened the waist and sometimes reached right down to the knees. Coats with huge fur collars were worn and evening wear consisted of sleeveless shift dresses, either in silver lamé or else covered in beading and fringing, and close-fitting beaded caps. Floppy pyjamas were all the rage for lounging in. Materials were supple and light and patterns were often geometrical, reflecting the fashion in the decorative arts. Although Paris remained the chief generator of these new styles, the long slim look was better adapted to the American or English physique. Hollywood films arriving from America helped to promote and spread the boyish styles, and links were established between the Parisian couturiers and Hollywood studios and stars. Fashion at all levels became big business, and the resulting enormous increase in publicity speeded up the evolution of fashion.

Much of the 1925 Exposition was devoted to fashion and in many ways the new styles reflected those emerging in interior design: simple and functional, barely ornamented or patterned geometrically, neatly shaped, and above all utterly modern and without precedent. And like the new furniture, the new styles of dress were also increasingly easy to mass produce.

This was a period when fashion was slowly becoming available to all women. As styles grew simpler, it became easier to copy models and make them at home, and large numbers of paper patterns were published in magazines. Chanel was one of the few couturiers who approved the fact that her designs were copied and made available to women of all classes. Now that dresses did not need to be fitted closely around hips and waist, ready-to-wear garments became available, mass-produced and machined. Because they were simpler and used less material, they were also cheaper to reproduce. The mass-produced clothes industry began really to take shape after the war. Fashion was gradually becoming a game all women could play, and those designers who

Opposite: 'A practical dress for the country'; the 1920s chemise dress.

Left: George Barbier and Paul Iribe's fan designs for the House of Paquin, 1912, showing the influence of Diaghiler's Ballets Russes.

Below: *Art, Goût, Beauté* fashion plate, 1921.

Right: 'Fashion for a windy day' by George Barbier from the *Gazette du Bon Ton*, c. 1925.

Opposite: A 1930s evening dress showing the popular black decolleté.

did not recognize that fact and adapt to it were soon ousted; Poiret was among those who refused to give up the idea of a fashion for the élite.

In the last years of the 1920s hems began to descend again, due in part to a reaction against the folly and excess of the previous years, and also to the generally more sober atmosphere brought on by the Depression. Evening dress hems began to swoop to floor level, at first dipping at the back to form an absurd little train, while day dresses were worn just above the ankle. In other respects the new fashions were forward-looking and innovative. Like the style that predominated in the decorative arts, they focused on clever manipulation of materials and the use of new synthetic fabrics. This softer, more feminine style was a reaction to the angularity and masculinity of the 1920s. Hair

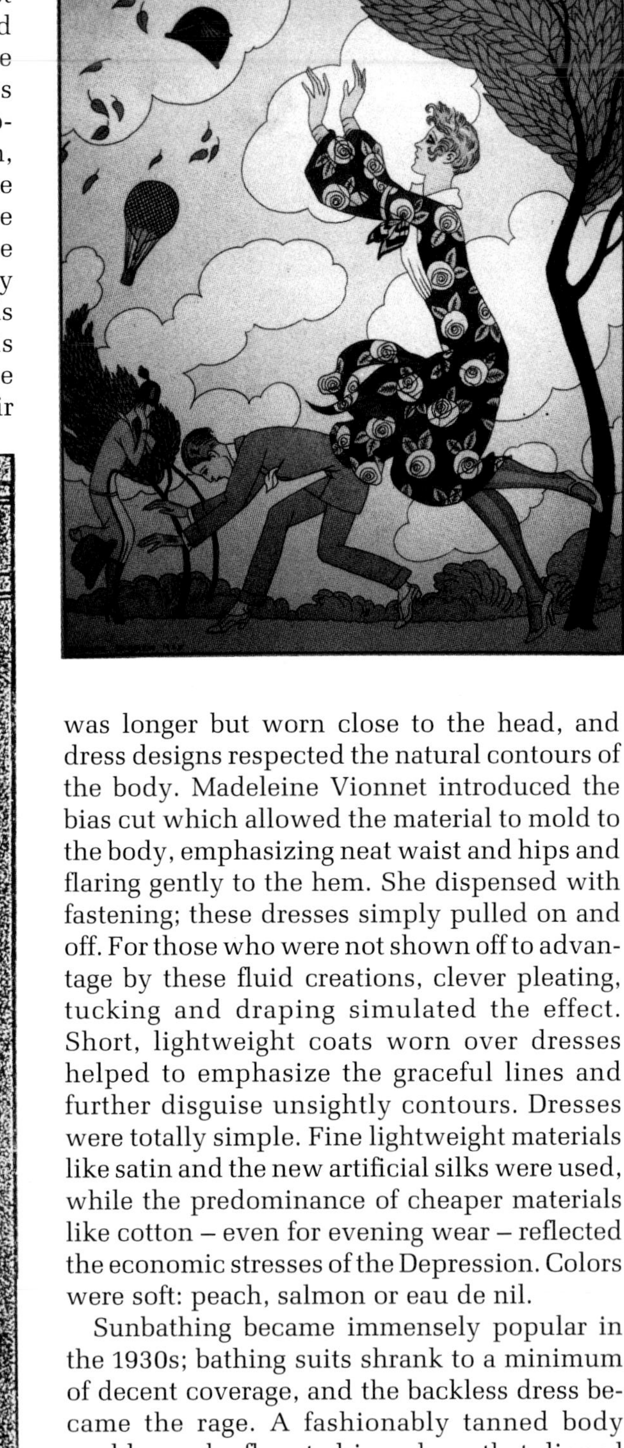

Below: Bathing fashions of the 1920s showing the fashionable boylike silhouette.

was longer but worn close to the head, and dress designs respected the natural contours of the body. Madeleine Vionnet introduced the bias cut which allowed the material to mold to the body, emphasizing neat waist and hips and flaring gently to the hem. She dispensed with fastening; these dresses simply pulled on and off. For those who were not shown off to advantage by these fluid creations, clever pleating, tucking and draping simulated the effect. Short, lightweight coats worn over dresses helped to emphasize the graceful lines and further disguise unsightly contours. Dresses were totally simple. Fine lightweight materials like satin and the new artificial silks were used, while the predominance of cheaper materials like cotton – even for evening wear – reflected the economic stresses of the Depression. Colors were soft: peach, salmon or eau de nil.

Sunbathing became immensely popular in the 1930s; bathing suits shrank to a minimum of decent coverage, and the backless dress became the rage. A fashionably tanned body could now be flaunted in a dress that dipped dramatically at the back. Long strings of beads, worn back to front, and embroidery and beading detailing enhanced the new cut.

As the Art Deco style began to wane, Elsa Schiaparelli came to the fore in fashion design. Fulfilling tendencies that had been apparent in other disciplines for some time, she introduced motifs derived from Cubism and Negro art into her designs. Then, from the mid-1930s she took fashion off in a new direction, developing a style inspired by Surrealism.

F.L.SCHMIED

When I'm stuck with a day that's gray and lonely,
I just stick out my chin and grim and say:

Oh! The sun'll come out tomorrow
So you got to hang on till tomorrow
Come what may!

Tomorrow, tomorrow, I love ya tomorrow,
You're always a day away.

Tomorrow, tomorrow, I love ya tomorrow,
You're always a day away.

Things to Think

BY ROBERT BLY

Think in ways you've never thought before
If the phone rings, think of it as carrying a message
Larger than anything you've ever heard,
Vaster than a hundred lines of Yeats.

Think that someone may bring a bear to your door,
Maybe wounded and deranged; or think that a moose
Has risen out of the lake, and he's carrying on his antlers
A child of your own whom you've never seen.

When someone knocks on the door, think that he's about
To give you something large: tell you you're forgiven,
Or that it's not necessary to work all the time, or that it's
Been decided that if you lie down no one will die.

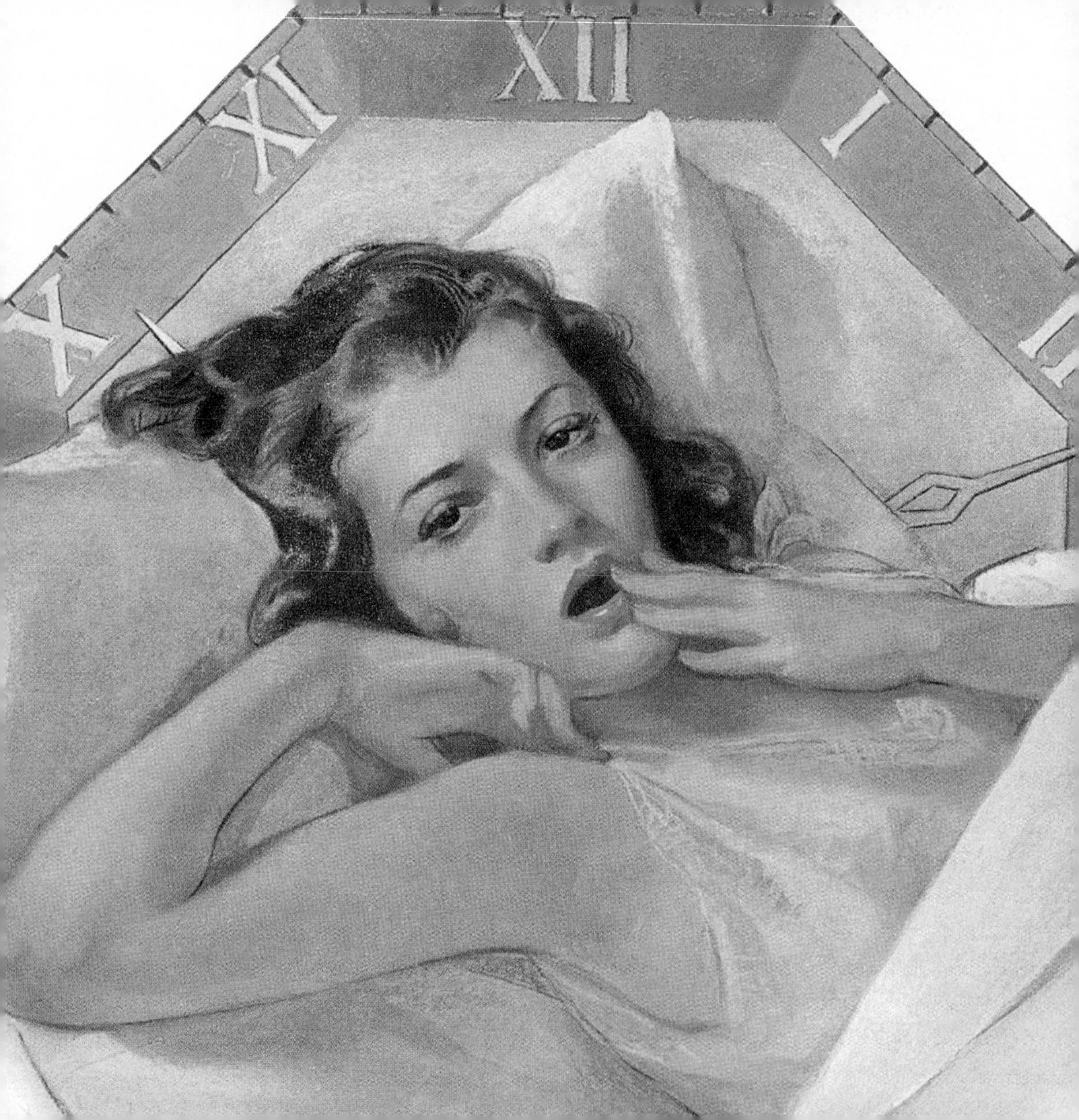

from "THE OCEAN" and "A VISION OF THE WORLD"

JOHN CHEEVER

...I AWOKE AT THREE, feeling terribly sad, and feeling rebelliously that I didn't want to study sadness, madness, melancholy, and despair. I wanted to study triumphs, the rediscoveries of love, all that I know in the world to be decent, radiant, and clear....

And I know that the sound of rain will wake some lovers, and that its sound will seem to be a part of that force that has thrust them into one another's arms. Then I sit up in bed and exclaim aloud to myself, "Valor! Love! Virtue! Compassion! Splendor! Kindness! Wisdom! Beauty!" The words seem to have the colors of the earth, and as I recite them I feel my hopefulness mount until I am contented and at peace with the night.

Poet Anne Sexton to Her 15-year-old Daughter Linda

April 1969

Wed — 2:45 P.M.
Dear Linda,
I am in the middle of a flight to St. Louis to give a reading. I was reading a NEW YORKER story that made me think of my mother and all alone in the seat I whispered to her "I know, Mother, I know." (Found a pen!) And I thought of you—someday flying somewhere all alone and me dead perhaps and you wishing to speak to me.

And I want to speak back. (Linda, maybe it won't be flying, maybe it will be at your OWN kitchen table drinking tea some afternoon when you are 40. ANYTIME.)—I want to say back.

1st I love you.
2. You never let me down.
3. I know. I was there once. I TOO, was 40 and with a dead mother who I needed still.

This is my message to the 40-year-old Linda. No matter what happens you were always my bobolink, my special Linda Gray. Life is

not easy. It is awfully lonely. I know that. Now you too know it—wherever you are, Linda, talking to me. But I've had a good life—I wrote unhappy—but I lived to the hilt. You too, Linda—Live to the HILT! To the top. I love you, 40-year-old Linda, and I love what you do, what you find, what you are!—Be your own woman. Belong to those you love. Talk to my poems, and talk to your heart—I'm in both: if you need me. I lied, Linda. I did love my mother and she loved me. She never held me but I miss her, so that I have to deny I ever loved her—or she me! Silly Anne! So there!

XOXOXO
Mom

I Will Survive

WORDS AND MUSIC BY DINO FEKARIS AND FREDDIE PERREN

At first I was afraid, I was petrified;
Kept thinkin' I could never live without you by my side.
But then, I spent so many nights thinkin' how you did me wrong
And I grew strong
And I learned how to get along.
And so you're back from outer space.
I just walk in to find you here with that sad look upon your face.
I should have change that stupid lock.
I should have made you leave your key,
if I'd've known for just one second you'd be back to bother me.

Go on now go, walk out the door;
Just turn around, now, 'cause you're not welcome any more.
Weren't you the one who tried to hurt me with good-bye?
Did you think I'd crumble,
Did you think I'd lay down and die.
Oh no, not I,
I will survive.
Oh as long as I know how to love,
I know I'll stay alive.
I've got all my life to live,
I've got all my love to give and I'll survive,
I will survive!

It took all the strength I had not to fall apart;
Kept tryin' hard to mend the pieces of my broken heart.
And I spent, oh, so many nights just feelin' sorry for myself,
I used to cry,
But now I hold my head up high.
And you see me,
Somebody new,
I'm not that chained up little person still in love with you.
And so you felt like droppin' in and just expect me to be free.
Well now, I'm savin' all my lovin' for someone who's lovin' me.

Go on now go, walk out the door;
Just turn around, now, 'cause you're not welcome any more.
Weren't you the one who tried to hurt me with good-bye?
Did you think I'd crumble,
did you think I'd lay down and die.
Oh no, not I,
I will survive.
Oh as long as I know how to love,
I know I'll stay alive.
I've got all my life to live,
I've got all my love to give and I'll survive,
I will survive!

It is the greatest shot of adrenaline to be doing what you've wanted to do so badly. You almost feel like you could fly without the plane.

CHARLES LINDBERGH

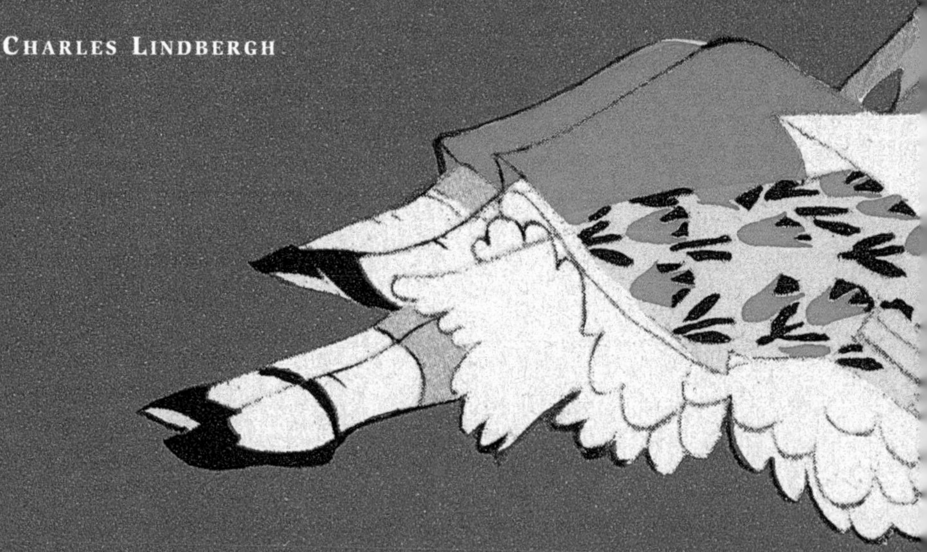

Leap Before You Look

BY W. H. AUDEN

The sense of danger must not disappear:
The way is certainly both short and steep,
However gradual it looks from here;
Look if you like, but you will have to leap.

Tough-minded men get mushy in their sleep
And break the by-laws any fool can keep;
It is not the convention but the fear
That has a tendency to disappear.

The worried efforts of the busy heap,
The dirt, the imprecision, and the beer
Produce a few smart wisecracks every year;
Laugh if you can, but you will have to leap.

The clothes that are considered right to wear
Will not be either sensible or cheap,
So long as we consent to live like sheep
And never mention those who disappear.

Much can be said for social savoir-faire,
But to rejoice when no one else is there
Is even harder than it is to weep;
No one is watching, but you have to leap.

A solitude ten thousand fathoms deep
Sustains the bed on which we lie, my dear:
Although I love you, you will have to leap;
Our dream of safety has to disappear.

CREATING BALANCE, HARMONY, AND SUCCESS: FENG SHUI

If you want to encourage change in your life,
move 27 things in your house.—Chinese Proverb

Are you drowning in a sea of clutter? Do you keep bumping into the furniture? Are your houseplants sickly? Do your windows need a good washing? Most people live with such imperfections everyday. But taken in combination, these exasperating flaws have the power to wear you down both physically and psychologically. Maybe it's time to get your house in order, literally. Feng Shui can help.

The 3,000-year-old practice of creating harmonious environments, Feng Shui (pronounced Fung Shway) centers on establishing the proper balance of Ch'i—the vital life-source that lives in and supports all things, animate and inanimate.

Traditional Feng Shui stresses balancing elements in your home using the principles of yin and yang and the five elements (Wood, Fire, Earth, Metal, and Water). It also employs what is called a

Bagua Map which helps you place items in "auspicious" locations in your house. But first, here are the three primary principles that govern the ancient Chinese art and philosophy. Their practical applications can be employed by anyone, and they are:

Everything is "alive."

Everything is connected.

Everything is constantly changing.

EVERYTHING IS ALIVE

How can understanding these principles be of any use to you? It's quite practical, really. If you accept that everything in your home contains life forces—your orchid, your pet goldfish, even your stapler—you will surround yourself with things that support your growth and sense of well-being. If 80 percent of the items you own are of no use to you, then it's time to make a change. Things you don't use or like hold negative energy, or Ch'i. They clutter your life, occupying valuable space in your home and mind. The simplest objects—family photographs, a scarf your sister knitted, a toothbrush—have value and therefore contain vital Ch'i. Paring down to the essentials can have a very cleansing effect, and help you to take better care of the things you love.

EVERYTHING IS CONNECTED

Understanding that all things are connected provides you with a holistic perspective. Living in a harmonious space offers peace of mind. A healthy environment has the power to lift your spirits and mind. If your home is a warm, comfortable place where you feel safe, you will certainly enjoy the time you spend there. Conversely, if your home is cluttered and disorganized (and you can never find your keys and wallet before you can leave the house), it can affect your punctuality, and therefore your job security, and therefore your financial standing, and therefore your family's welfare, and therefore your health. This may seem like an exaggerated example, but the simplest things can have a large impact when we are habitually associated with them.

EVERYTHING IS CONSTANTLY CHANGING

It may surprise you to learn that maintaining a harmonious environment doesn't mean that you can "fix" your house once and never change it again. Since you are continually evolving with ever-changing goals, desires, and tastes, your environment should change to support your growth. For example, when you move, your inevitably get rid of things that are no longer useful. Or, when you return from vacation or a business trip, you are inspired to make changes in your home from something you learned while you were away.

If you are interested in delving deeper into the art of Feng Shui, then understanding the principles of the Bagua is essential. The Feng Shui Bagua Map stems from the *I Ching* (*The Book of Changes*) by Lao Tzu. Bagua refers to the eight essential energies or treasures in the universe that govern our lives. When applied to Feng Shui, the Bagua Map can be used to discover which parts of your home correspond to the different areas of your life. On the following page is an example of a Bagua Map:

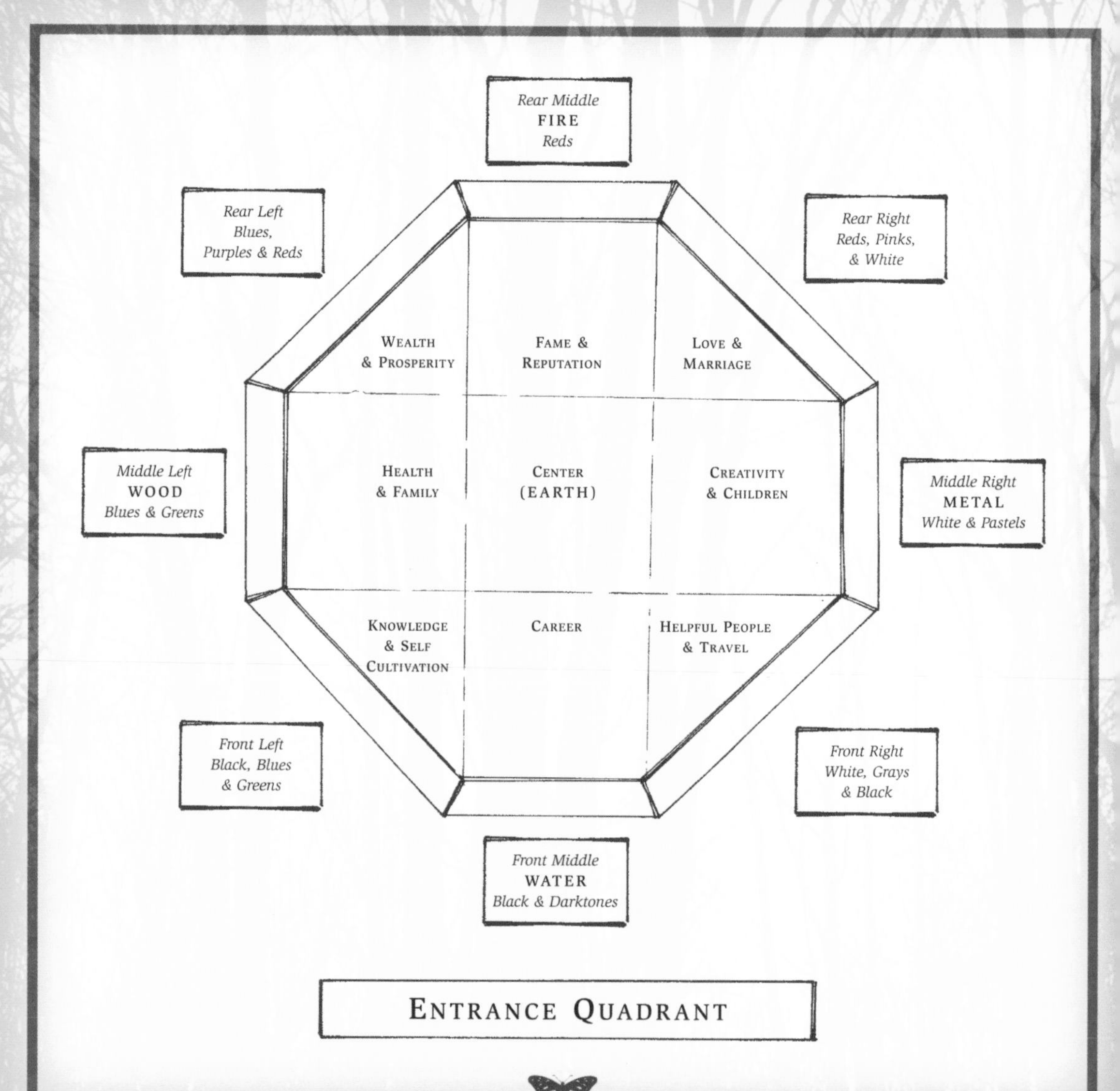
Rear Middle
FIRE
Reds
Rear Left
Blues,
Purples & Reds
Rear Right
Reds, Pinks,
& White
Wealth
& Prosperity
Fame &
Reputation
Love &
Marriage
Middle Left
WOOD
Blues & Greens
Health
& Family
Center
(EARTH)
Creativity
& Children
Middle Right
METAL
White & Pastels
Knowledge
& Self
Cultivation
Career
Helpful People
& Travel
Front Left
Black, Blues
& Greens
Front Right
White, Grays
& Black
Front Middle
WATER
Black & Darktones
Entrance Quadrant

Now, imagine you have a bird's-eye view of your home or apartment. If you were to place a Bagua Map directly over your dwelling—aligning the Entrance Quadrant with your front door—you could see which "corners" correspond to the various treasures.

Using the color and element coding of the Bagua, you can beautify your respective corners, thereby enhancing the overall Ch'i of your space. Colors can be conveyed with the use of paint, art, upholstery, etc. You may also wish to place symbolic objects in each area (e.g., a goldfish in a clean aquarium will enhance your Career corner). Above all else, make sure you love all the objects and colors used for the enhancements. If you use an object or color you don't like just because it matches the criteria for your corner, it will fail to have the desired effect.

So what if your dwelling is not shaped like a square (most spaces aren't), and some of the "corners" on your map extend beyond your exterior walls? For example, the "Children & Creativity" corner of your house may be missing. What do you do? First off, don't panic! If it extends into your yard or patio, you can use that outdoor space as your corner. Simply use white and pastel flowers, and place a whimsical sculpture of children or other representative object in that area. Using outdoor lighting can also anchor a missing corner. If you don't have access or control over the space that would finish off your corner, you can still enhance the energy of that area, or "fix" the flow of Ch'i inside your space. This can be achieved with the use of plants, mirrors, and crystals. Placing a mirror on one or two of the walls will make the indentation seem to disappear. If there are windows on one or two walls, you can hang a round crystal in a window and place a beautiful plant nearby to stimulate and circulate the Ch'i.

Once you've successfully worked with your structure as a whole, you may wish to use the Bagua to map your individual rooms. Don't feel as though you need to deal with every room in order to get it right. Start with the rooms that represent the areas of your life you wish to enhance. Again, use the entrance as your key for orienting the Bagua Map. If there are two doors, use the one that is most frequently used.

FENG SHUI ESSENTIALS:

The kitchen in your home, no matter the location, represents your financial well-being. A clean kitchen is therefore very important: in particular, the stove.

Obtrusive corners, interior columns, or bulky furniture in the center of a room can easily block the flow of Ch'i. This is sometimes hard to avoid in a large, open space. You can fix this problem by dissecting a room visually.

In general, square items hold energy while round items move energy along.

Always keep bathroom doors and the toilet-seat lids closed. This avoids having your luck or money "go down the toilet."

Mirrors can unblock stagnant energy. But be careful that the rest of the room you are placing a mirror in is harmonious. Mirrors can "double" other imbalances.

No one likes to be stared at, and your television can act as an enormous black eye watching your every move. Cover or conceal all televisions either with a cloth or inside a cabinet.

Lighting can enhance the Ch'i of any room. Lights that point up can "fix" a low ceiling. Fluorescent lighting, however, has the reverse effect. It depletes Ch'i with its flicker and its limited light spectrum. Use incandescent or halogen lights whenever possible. Fitting fluorescent fixtures with full-spectrum bulbs can also be helpful—though the problem of flickering light still remains.

It is a good idea to place a wind chime, bells, or a music box in areas such as "Career," "Love," or "Creativity." Pleasing sounds welcome Ch'i and create new opportunities.

Water features also generate pleasing sounds. They can stimulate the Ch'i in any area you wish to enhance.

It stands to reason that people who live in comfortable surroundings live happier, healthier, more productive lives. The time it takes to create your peaceful home is time well spent. Even if your living situation is temporary, that's no excuse! Nurture yourself now.

The Green Stream

Wang Wei

To get to the yellow flower river
I always follow the green water stream
Among the hills there must be a thousand twists
The distance there cannot be fifty miles
There is the murmur of water among rocks
And the quietness of colors deep in pines
Lightly, lightly drifting water-chestnuts
Clearly, clearly mirrored reeds and rushes
I have always been lover of tranquility
And when I see this clear stream so calm
I want to stay on some great rock
And sit forever on and on.

This is your life, not someone else's. It is your own feeling of what is important, not what people will say. Sooner or later, you are bound to discover that you cannot please all of the people around you all of the time. Some of them will attribute to you motives you never dreamed of. Some of them will misinterpret your words and actions, making them completely alien to you. So you had better learn fairly early that you must not expect to have everyone understand what you say and what you do. The important thing is to be sure that those who love you, whether family or friends, understand as nearly as you can make them understand. If they believe in you, they will trust your motives. But do not ask or expect to have anyone with you on everything. Do not try for it. To reach such a state of unanimity would mean that you would risk losing your own individuality to attain it.

ELEANOR ROOSEVELT

ZEN AND THE ART OF MOTORCYCLE MAINTENANCE

By Robert Pirsig

Mountains should be climbed with as little effort as possible and without desire. The reality of your own nature should determine the speed. If you become restless, speed up. If you become winded, slow down. You climb the mountain in an equilibrium between restlessness and exhaustion. Then, when you're no longer thinking ahead, each footstep isn't just a means to an end but a unique event in itself. *This* leaf has jagged edges. *This* rock looks loose. From *this* place the snow is less visible, even though closer. These are things you should notice anyway. To live only for some future goal is shallow. It's the sides of the mountain which sustain life, not the top. Here's where things grow.

But of course, without the top you can't have any sides. It's the top that *defines* the sides. So on we go...we have a long way . . . no hurry . . . just one step after the next...with a little Chautauqua for entertainment....Mental reflection is so much more interesting than TV it's a shame more people don't switch over to it. They probably think what they hear is unimportant but it never is.

Photographer Ansel Adams to his friend, Cedric Wright

June 10, 1937

Dear Cedric,

A strange thing happened to me today. I saw a big thundercloud move down over Half Dome, and it was so big and clear and brilliant that it made me see many things that were drifting around inside of me; things that related to those who are loved and those who are real friends.

For the first time I KNOW what love is; what friends are; and what art should be.

Love is a seeking for a way of life; the way that cannot be followed alone; the resonance of all spiritual and physical things. Children are not only of flesh and blood—children may be ideas, thoughts, emotions. The person of the one who is loved is a form composed of a myriad mirrors reflecting and illuminating the powers and the thoughts and the emotions that are within you, and flashing another kind of light from within. No words or deeds may encompass it.

Friendship is another form of love—more passive perhaps, but full of the transmitting and acceptance of things like thunderclouds and grass and the clean reality of granite.

Art is both love and friendship, and understanding; the desire to give. It is not charity, which is the giving of Things, it is more than kindness which is the giving of self. It is both the taking and giving of beauty, the turning out to the light the inner folds of the awareness of the spirit. It is the recreation on another plane of the realities of the world; the tragic and wonderful realities of earth and men, and of all the inter-relations of these.

I wish the thundercloud had moved up over Tahoe and let loose on you; I could wish you nothing finer.

Ansel

TONI MORRISON

SARAH LAWRENCE COLLEGE, MAY 27, 1988

I WANT TO TALK ABOUT the activity you are always warned against as being wasteful, impractical, hopeless. I want to talk about dreaming.... We are in a mess, you know, and we have to get out....

Well, now, you may be asking yourself, "What is all of this? I can't save the world. What about my life? I didn't come here for this. I didn't even ask to come here. I didn't ask to be born." Didn't you? I put it to you that you did. You not only asked to be born, you insisted on your life. That's why you're here. There's no other reason. It's too easy not to have been born, and now that you're here, you have to do something. Something you respect, don't you? Your parents may have wanted you, but they did not dream you up. You did that. I'm just urging you to continue the dream you started, because dreaming is not irresponsible. It's first order, human business. It's not entertainment, you know. It's work. When Martin Luther King said, "I have a dream," he wasn't playing; he was serious. When he imagined it, envisioned, created it in his own mind, it began. Now we have to dream it too and give it the heft and stretch and longevity it deserves, but don't let anybody convince you this is the way the world is and therefore must be. It must be the way it ought to be. . . .

You are not helpless and you're not heartless, and you have time. Thank you.

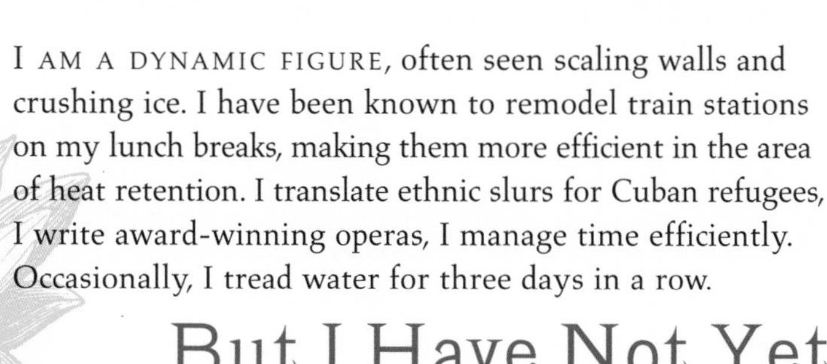

I AM A DYNAMIC FIGURE, often seen scaling walls and crushing ice. I have been known to remodel train stations on my lunch breaks, making them more efficient in the area of heat retention. I translate ethnic slurs for Cuban refugees, I write award-winning operas, I manage time efficiently. Occasionally, I tread water for three days in a row.

But I Have Not Yet Gone to College

HUGH GALLAGHER

I woo women with my sensuous and godlike trombone playing, I can pilot bicycles up severe inclines with unflagging speed, and I cook Thirty-Minute Brownies in twenty minutes. I am an expert in stucco, a veteran in love, and an outlaw in Peru.

Using only a hoe and a large glass of water, I once single-handedly defended a small village in the Amazon Basin from a horde of ferocious army ants. I play bluegrass cello, I was scouted by the Mets, I am the subject of numerous documentaries. When I'm bored, I build large suspension bridges in my yard. I enjoy urban hang gliding. On Wednesdays, after school, I repair electrical appliances free of charge.

I am an abstract artist, a concrete analyst, and a ruthless bookie. Critics worldwide swoon over my original line of corduroy evening wear. I don't perspire. I am a private citizen, yet I receive fan mail. I have been caller number nine and have won the weekend passes. Last summer I toured New Jersey with a traveling centrifugal-force demonstration. I bat .400. My deft floral arrangements have earned me fame in international botany circles. Children trust me.

I can hurl tennis rackets at small moving objects with deadly accuracy. I once read *Paradise Lost, Moby Dick,* and *David Copperfield* in one day and still had time to refurbish an entire dining room that evening. I know the exact location of every food item in the supermarket. I have performed several covert operations for the CIA. I sleep once a week; when I do sleep, I sleep in a chair. While on vacation in Canada, I successfully negotiated with a group of terrorists who had seized a small bakery. The laws of physics do not apply to me.

I balance, I weave, I dodge, I frolic, and my bills are all paid. On weekends, to let off steam, I participate in full-contact origami. Years ago I discovered the meaning of life but forgot to write it down. I have made extraordinary four course meals using only a mouli and a toaster oven. I breed prize-winning clams. I have won bullfights in San Juan, cliff-diving competitions in Sri Lanka, and spelling bees at the Kremlin. I have played Hamlet, I have performed open-heart surgery, and I have spoken with Elvis.

But I have not yet gone to college.

Forever Young

WORDS AND MUSIC BY BOB DYLAN

May God bless and keep you always
May your wishes all come true
May you always do for others
And let others do for you.

May you build a ladder to the stars
And climb on ev'ry rung
May you stay forever young.
Forever young
Forever young
May you stay forever young.

May you grow up to be righteous
May you grow up to be true
May you always know the truth
And see the lights surrounding you.

May you always be courageous
Stand up right and be strong
May you stay forever young.
Forever young
Forever young
May you stay
Forever young.

May your hands always be busy
May your feet always be swift
May you have a strong foundation
When the winds of changes shift.
May your heart always be joyful
May your song always be sung
May you stay forever young.

PSALM 23:1–7

King James Bible

A Psalm of David. The LORD is my shepherd; I shall not want.

He maketh me to lie down in green pastures: he leadeth me beside the still waters.

He restoreth my soul: he leadeth me in the paths of righteousness for his name's sake.

Yea, though I walk through the valley of the shadow of death, I will fear no evil: for thou art with me; thy rod and thy staff they comfort me.

Thou preparest a table before me in the presence of mine enemies: thou anointest my head with oil; my cup runneth over.

Surely goodness and mercy shall follow me all the days of my life: and I will dwell in the house of the LORD for ever.

From **Leaves of Grass**

By Walt Whitman

Has any one supposed it lucky to be born?
I hasten to inform him or her it is
just as lucky to die, and I know it.

I pass death with the dying and birth
with the new-wash'd babe, and am not
contain'd between my hat and boots,
And peruse manifold objects,
no two alike and every one good,
The earth good and the stars good,
and their adjuncts all good.

I am not an earth nor an adjunct
of an earth,
I am the mate and companion of people,
all just as immortaland fathomless
as myself,
(They do not know how immortal,
but I know.)

Every kind for itself and its own,
for me mine male and female,
For me those that have been boys
and that love women,
For me the man that is proud and feels
how it stings to be slighted,
For me the sweet-heart and the old maid,
for me mothers
and the mothers of mothers,
For me lips that have smiled,
eyes that have shed tears,
For me children and the begetters
of children.

COLIN POWELL

Fisk University
May 4, 1992

...WHAT WE MUST NEVER LOSE is faith. Faith that in the end right will prevail. Faith in the basic goodness of America and in the basic goodness of Americans.

We must remember that America is a family. There may be differences and disputes in our family but we must not allow the family to be broken into warring factions.

In a few moments you will become members of that family. Here's what I want you to do.

First, I want you to believe in yourself. You have to know that you are capable, that you are competent, that you are good. Your family and Fisk University have seen to that. But *you* have to believe it. I want you to believe that there is nothing—NOTHING—you cannot accomplish by hard work and commitment. Let nothing or no one ever destroy that belief you have in yourself.

Second, I want you to believe in America with all your heart, with all your mind, with all your soul, and with all your body. I've traveled around this world, and I've seen a hundred countries, and I've got to tell you there is no better place or system on earth than that which we enjoy here in America.

America is the hope and promise of the world. We are still, as Abraham Lincoln said, "the last, best hope of earth."

Third, I want you to find strength in your diversity. Let the fact that you are black or yellow or white be a source of pride and inspiration to you. Draw strength from it. Let it be someone else's problem, but never yours. Never hide behind it or use it as an excuse for not doing your best.

We all have to live here together—Asian Americans, African Americans, Hispanic Americans, all of us.

Divided, fighting amongst ourselves, walking separate lines of diversity, we are as weak as newborn babies.

Together, intertwining our many differences and diversities into a mosaic of strength, we will prevail over the darkness of racism. I want you to love one another, I want you to respect one another, see the best in each other. Share each other's pain and joy.

I want you to fight racism. I want you to rail against it. We have to make sure that it bleeds to death in this country once and for all.

As you move forward, I want you to remember those who are still struggling. We must reach back, we must all reach down, we must all work together to pull our people, to pull all Americans out of the violence, out of the dank and soul-damning world of drugs, out of the turmoil of our inner cities. As we climbed on the backs of others, so must we allow our backs to be used for others to go even higher than we have.

Finally, I want you to raise strong families. I want you to create families and raise children who are God-fearing, who are loving, who are clean, and who are determined to do even better than their parents.

As you raise your families, remember the worst kind of poverty is not economic poverty; it is the poverty of *values*. It is the poverty of *caring*. It is the poverty of *love*.

The other evening Alma and I were privileged to be with Maya Angelou. She talked about her upbringing in Stamp, Arkansas. She told us something her grandmother had said to her many years ago. Her grandmother had said, "Girl, when you cross this threshold, you're going to be *raised*."

So raise your children. Treasure them. Love them. They are our future. We cannot let the generation in front of us go to waste.

To look out at you gives me enormous hope. You look so competent, so strong, so young, so committed, so ready to take on the future, difficult times and all.

Looking at you gives me the same feeling of pride that I get when I look at our soldiers, our sailors, our airmen and marines and coast guardsmen. I know when I see them that there is nothing they can't handle, no difficulty they can't overcome, no challenge they don't relish, no mission they can't perform.

Very soon you too will be soldiers. Soldiers in the exciting struggle of life. Soldiers for education. Soldiers for business. Soldiers for science. And, above all, soldiers for a better America.

I believe in this great land that God blessed and called America—because it is full of young men and women like you. Men and women who will keep this nation moving on down the road to glory, its beacon of freedom lighting up all the dark places of the world until there is no darkness left.

We're counting on you! We're counting on you!

Don't go around saying the world owes you a living; the world owes you nothing; it was here first.

MARK TWAIN

GIVING BACK

If you want happiness
for an hour—take a nap.
If you want happiness
for a day—go fishing.
If you want happiness
for a month—get married.
If you want happiness
for a year—inherit a fortune.
If you want happiness
for a lifetime—help someone else.

—Chinese proverb

Most of us spend the first couple decades of our life wondering: who am I? We spend our early, sometimes angst-riddled, years searching for our identity. It is the next question, however, that can plague us until our dying day: What is my purpose in life? This question usually comes on the heels of our discovery that money isn't everything, work outside the home will end, and that we are not the only person in the universe. It is the quest to answer this question—and not necessarily the answer itself—that can strengthen our character and increase our integrity.

Discovering that the effort we exert in life doesn't always have to involve a money-making venture is a great first step. Next, we learn that our talents can be used to better the lives of those in our personal sphere. Some of us stop there—content to "give back" by helping and caring for our friends and family (a noble cause in itself). But what if we extended our notion of giving back to include problems and people beyond our personal sphere?

Albert Einstein, in his book *The Human Side*, calls for a "widening of our circle of compassion to embrace all living creatures and the whole of nature in its beauty." It sounds like heavy stuff, but it doesn't need to be.

Einstein's command can be achieved in large ways (by mentoring, teaching, volunteering, and donating) or small (by being a courteous driver, giving blood, helping a friend in need, and picking up someone else's litter off the street). So, next time you see a stranger who appears to be having a bad day, smile.

Donate time to the local Parks Department. Become a troop leader for your community's chapter of the Girl/Boy Scouts of America. Volunteer at the area Women's Shelter. Operate the local Help Line/Crisis Line. At the very least, vote in every election for which you are eligible. Or give your time or money to the following organizations:

American Civil Liberties Union (ACLU):
www.aclu.org
125 Broad Street, 18th Floor
New York, New York 10004
212-549-2555
212-549-2648 FAX
National organization dedicated to upholding the Bill of Rights.

Big Brothers Big Sisters of America:
www.bbbsa.org
230 North Thirteenth Street
Philadelphia, PA 19107-1538
215-567-7000
215-567-0394 FAX
National organization that pairs adult volunteers with at-risk youth.

Habitat for Humanity International:
www.habitat.org
121 Habitat Street
Americus, GA 31709-3498
800-HABITAT (800-422-4828, ext. 2551 or 2552
229-924-6935
International organization that works to build or rehabilitate houses for families in need.

Human Rights Watch: www.hrw.org
350 Fifth Avenue
New York, New York, 10118
212-290-4700
212-736-1300 FAX
International organization that seeks to defend human rights worldwide.

Meals on Wheels Association of America:
www.projectmeal.org
1414 Prince Street, Suite 302
Alexandria, Virginia 22314
703-548-5558
National organization that provides home-delivered meal services to people in need.

OXFAM
26 West Street
Boston, MA 02111
800-77OXFAM
617-728-2596 FAX
International organization dedicated to fighting hunger through funding long-term development and disaster relief projects in 28 countries throughout Africa, Asia, the Americas, and the Caribbean.

Proliteracy Worldwide: www.proliteracy.org
1320 Jamesville Avenue
Syracuse, NY 13210
800-448-8878 (Catalog orders ONLY)
315-422-9121
315-472-0002 FAX
National organization that works on a local level to provide adult literacy education.

Save the Children: www.savechildren.net
54 Wilton Road
Westport, CT 06881
800-729-1446
203-221-4000
203-221-4077 FAX
Organization that helps children in need in the United States as well as in more than 50 other countries.

Tails a' Waggin' Rescue: www.animalrescue.in-motion.net
P.O. Box 37
Whitestown, IN 46075
317-769-2543
317-769-4007 FAX
A non-profit animal rescue organization for abandoned, homeless, and abused animals.

Teach for America:
www.teachforamerica.org
National Office
315 West 36th Street
New York, NY 10018
800-832-1230
212-279-2080
212-279-2081 FAX
National organization that places recent college graduates into 2-year teaching assignments in public schools located in low-income areas.

Three things in human
life are important:
the first is to be kind.
The second is to be kind.
The third is to be kind.

HENRY JAMES

A Coat

BY WILLIAM BUTLER YEATS

I made my song a coat

Covered with embroideries

Out of old mythologies

From heel to throat;

But the fools caught it,

Wore it in the world's eyes

As though they'd wrought it.

Song, let them take it,

For there's more enterprise

In walking naked.

AUTHOR AYN RAND TO HER FAN, JOANNE RONDEAU

MAY 22, 1948

Dear Ms. Rondeau:

You asked me to explain the meaning of my sentence in THE FOUNTAINHEAD: "To say 'I love you' one must know first how to say the 'I.'"

The meaning of that sentence is contained in the whole of THE FOUNTAINHEAD. And it is stated right in the speech on page 400 from which you took that sentence. The meaning of the "I" is an independent, self-sufficient entity that DOES NOT EXIST for the sake of any other person.

A person who exists only for the sake of his loved one is not an independent entity, but a spiritual parasite. The love of a parasite is worth nothing.

The usual (and very vicious) nonsense preached on the subject of love claims that love is self-sacrifice. A man's SELF *is his spirit. If one sacrifices his spirit, who or what is left to feel the love? True love is profoundly* SELFISH, *in the noblest meaning of the word—it is an expression of one's* SELF, *of one's highest values. When a person is in love, he seeks his own happiness—and* NOT *his sacrifice to the loved one. And the loved one would be a monster if she wanted or expected sacrifice.*

Any person who wants to live FOR *others—for one sweetheart or for the whole of mankind—is a selfless nonentity. An independent "I" is a person who exists for his own sake. Such a person does not make any vicious pretense of self-sacrifice and does not demand it from the person he loves. Which is the only way to be in love and the only form of a self-respecting relationship between two people.*

Blackbird

BY JOHN LENNON AND PAUL MCCARTNEY

Blackbird singing in the dead of night
Take these broken wings and learn to fly;
All your life you were only waiting for this moment to arise.
Blackbird, fly,
Blackbird, fly, into the light of a dark, black night.

Blackbird, fly,
Blackbird, fly,
into the light of a dark, black night.

Blackbird singing in the dead of night
Take these broken wings and learn to fly;
All your life
You were only waiting for this moment to arise,
You were only waiting for this moment to arise

Blackbird singing in the dead of night
Take these sunken eyes and learn to see;
All your life
you were only waiting for this moment to be free.
Blackbird, fly,
Blackbird, fly, into the light of a dark, black night.

Blackbird, fly,
Blackbird, fly,
into the light of a dark, black night.

Blackbird singing in the dead of night
Take these broken wings and learn to fly;
All your life
You were only waiting for this moment to arise,
You were only waiting for this moment to arise.

Tomorrow hopes we have learned something from yesterday.

JOHN WAYNE

from PERSONAL NARRATIVE

JONATHAN EDWARDS

...I WALKED ABROAD ALONE, in a solitary place in my father's pasture for contemplation. And as I was walking there, and looking upon the sky and clouds, there came into my mind so sweet a sense of the glorious majesty and grace of God, as I know not how to express.—I seemed to see them both in a sweet conjunction; majesty and meekness joined together; it was a sweet and gentle and holy majesty; and also a majestic meekness, a high and great, and holy gentleness.

After this my sense of divine things gradually increased, and became more and more lively, and had more of that inward sweetness. The appearance of every thing was altered; there seemed to be, as it were, a calm, sweet cast, or appearance of divine glory, in almost every thing... in the sun, moon, and stars; in the clouds and blue sky, in the grass, flowers, trees; in the water and all nature.... I often used to sit and view the moon for a long time; and in the day, spent much time in viewing the clouds and sky, to behold the sweet glory of God in these things.... Before, I used to be uncommonly terrified with thunder, and to be struck with terror when I saw a thunder-storm rising; but now, on the contrary, it rejoiced me. I felt God, if I may so speak, at the first appearance of a thunder-storm; and used to take the opportunity, at such time, to fix myself in order to view the clouds, and see the lightnings play.... While thus engaged, it always seemed natural for me to sing, or chant forth meditations; or to speak my thoughts in soliloquies with a singing voice.

Ode 1.9/To Thaliarchus

BY HORACE

See Mount Soracte shining in the snow.
See how the laboring overladen trees
Can scarcely bear their burdens
  any longer.

See how the streams are frozen
  in the cold.
Bring in the wood and light the fire
  and open
The fourth-year vintage wine
  in the Sabine jars.

O Thaliarchus, as for everything else,
Forget tomorrow. Leave it up to the gods.
Once the gods have decided,
  the winds at sea
Will quiet down, and the sea
  will quiet down,
And these cypresses and old
  ash trees will shake
In the storm no longer.
  Take everything as it comes.

Put down in your books
  as profit every new day
That Fortune allows you to have.
  While you're still young,
And while morose old age is far away,

There's love, there are parties,
  there's dancing and there's music,
There are young people out
  in the city squares together
As evening comes on, there are
  whispers of lovers, there's laughter.

We are all in the gutter,
but some of us are
looking at the stars.
Oscar Wilde

THE DEVELOPMENT of my philosophy came about as follows: My wife, inviting me to sample her very first soufflé, accidentally dropped a spoonful of it on my foot, fracturing several small bones. Doctors were called in, X-rays taken and examined, and I was ordered to bed for a month. During this convalescence, I turned to the works of some of Western society's most formidable thinkers—a stack of books I had laid aside for just such an eventuality. Scorning chronological order, I began with Kierkegaard

My Philosophy

BY WOODY ALLEN

and Sartre, then moved quickly to Spinoza, Hume, Kafka, and Camus. I was not bored, as I had feared I might be; rather, I found myself fascinated by the alacrity with which these great minds unflinchingly attacked morality, art, ethics, life, and death. I remembered my reaction to a typically luminous observation of Kierkegaard's: "Such a relation which relates itself to its own self (that is to say, a self) must either have constituted itself or have been constituted by another." The concept brought tears to my eyes. My word, I thought, to be that clever! (I'm a man who has trouble writing two meaningful sentences on "My Day at the Zoo.") True, the passage was totally incomprehensible to me, but what of it as long as Kierkegaard was having fun? Suddenly confident that metaphysics was the work I had always been meant to do, I took up my pen and began at once to jot down the first of my own musings. The work proceeded apace, and in a mere two afternoons—with time out for dozing and trying to get the two little BBs into the eyes of the bear—I had completed the philosophical work that I am hoping will not be uncovered until after my death, or until the year 3000 (whichever comes first), and which I modestly believe will assure me a place of reverence among history's weightiest thinkers. Here is but a small sample of the main body of intellectual treasure that I leave for posterity, or until the cleaning woman comes.

I. Critique of Pure Dread

In formulating any philosophy, the first consideration must always be: What can we know? That is, what can we be sure we know, or sure that we know we knew it, if indeed it is at all knowable. Or have we simply forgotten it and are too embarrassed to say anything? Descartes hinted at the problem when he wrote, "My mind can never know my body, although it has become quite friendly with my legs." By "knowable," incidentally, I do not mean that which can be known by perception of the senses, or that which can be grasped by the mind, but more that which can be said to be Known or to possess a Knownness or Knowability, or at least something you can mention to a friend.

Can we actually "know" the universe? My God, it's hard enough finding your way around in Chinatown.

The point, however, is: Is there anything out there? And why? And must they be so noisy? Finally, there can be no doubt that the one characteristic of "reality" is that it lacks essence. That is not to say it has no essence, but merely lacks it. (The reality I speak of here is the same one Hobbes described, but a little smaller.) Therefore the Cartesian dictum "I think, therefore I am" might better be expressed "Hey, there goes Edna with a saxophone!" So, then, to know a substance or an idea we must doubt it, and thus, doubting it, come to perceive the qualities it possesses in its finite state, which are truly "in the thing itself," or "of the thing itself," or of something or nothing. If this is clear, we can leave epistemology for the moment.

II. Eschatological Dialectics As a Means of Coping with Shingles

We can say that the universe consists of a substance, and this substance we will call "atoms," or else we will call it "monads." Democritus called it atoms. Liebnitz called it monads. Fortunately, the two men never met, or there would have been a very dull argument. These "particles" were set in motion by some cause or underlying principle, or perhaps something fell someplace. The point is that it's too late to do anything about it now, except possibly to eat plenty of raw fish. This, of course, does not explain why the soul is immortal. Nor does it say anything about an afterlife, or about the feeling my uncle Sender has that he is being followed by Albanians. The causal relationship between the first principle (i.e., God, or a strong wind) and any teleological concept of being (Being) is, according to Pascal, "so ludicrous that it's not even funny (Funny)." Schopenhauer called this "will," but his physician diagnosed it as hay fever. In his later years, he became embittered by it, or more likely because of his increasing suspicion that he was not Mozart.

III. The Cosmos on Five Dollars a Day

What, then, is "beautiful"? The merging of harmony with the just, or the merging of harmony with something that just sounds like "the just"? Possibly harmony should have been merged with "the crust" and this is what's been giving us our trouble. Truth, to be sure, is beauty— or "the necessary." That is, what is good or possessing the qualities of "the good" results in "truth." If it doesn't, you can bet the thing is not beautiful, although it may still be waterproof. I am beginning to think I was right in the first place and that everything should be merged with the crust. Oh, well.

Two Parables

A man approaches a palace. Its only entrance is guarded by some fierce Huns who will only let men named Julius enter. The man tries to bribe the guards by offering them a year's supply of choice chicken parts. They neither scorn his offer nor accept it, but merely take his nose and twist it till it looks like a Molly screw. The man says it is imperative that he enter the palace because he is bringing the emperor a change of underwear. When the guards still refuse, the man begins to Charleston. They seem to enjoy his dancing but soon become morose over the treatment of the Navajos by the federal government. Out of breath, the man collapses. He dies, never having seen the emperor and owing the Steinway people sixty dollars on a piano he had rented from them in August.

I am given a message to deliver to a general. I ride and ride, but the general's headquarters seem to get farther and farther away. Finally, a giant black panther leaps upon me and devours my mind and heart. This puts a terrific crimp in my evening. No matter how hard I try, I cannot catch the general, whom I see running in the distance in his shorts and whispering the word "nutmeg" to his enemies.

Aphorisms

It is impossible to experience one's own death objectively and still carry a tune.

The universe is merely a fleeting idea in God's mind—a pretty uncomfortable thought, particularly if you've just made a down payment on a house.

Eternal nothingness is O.K. if you're dressed for it.

If only Dionysus were alive! Where would he eat?

Not only is there no God, but try getting a plumber on weekends.

SAFETY
FIRST

Somehow I can't believe that there are any heights that can't be scaled by a man who knows the secrets of making dreams come true. This special secret, it seems to me, can be summarized in four C's. They are curiosity, confidence, courage, and constancy, and the greatest of all is confidence. When you believe in a thing, believe in it all the way, implicitly and unquestionably.

WALT DISNEY

Look for the Silver Lining

BY JEROME KERN

Please don't be offended
    if I preach to you a while,
Tears are out of place in eyes
    that were meant to smile.
There's a way to make your
    very biggest troubles small,
Here's the happy secret of it all:

CHORUS
Look for the silver lining
Whene'er a cloud appears in the blue.
Remember somewhere the sun is shining
And so the right thing to do is make it
    shine for you.
A heart full of joy and gladness
Will always banish sadness and strife
So always look for the silver lining
And try to find the sunny side of life.

As I wash my dishes, I'll be following
    your plan,
Till I see the brightness in ev'ry pot and
    pan.
I am sure your point of view will ease
    the daily grind,
So I'll keep repeating in my mind:

(CHORUS)

CARL SAGAN

WHEATON COLLEGE
MAY 20, 1993

...WE OWE OUR LIVES—not just the quality of our lives, but the existence of our lives—to technology. Most people on earth would be dead if not for modern agriculture and modern medicine. At the same time, that technology permits weapons of mass destruction, permits inadvertent changes in the environment that sustains us all.

Clearly before us is the very dicey job of using these enormous powers wisely. This is something that we haven't had much experience in because we've never had powers this great. The capability both for good and for evil is unexcelled. And that means that this generation—you young women and men—has an absolute key role to play in the long adventure of the human species.

Because of the newness of co-education...I want to share a few thoughts with you....We are very close relatives of the chimpanzees. We share 99.6 percent of active genes with chimpanzees, which means there's a lot about us we can learn from chimps. Now it's clear that chimp society is—how shall I say?—testosterone ridden. By no means all, but a great deal of the aggression and intimidation is something the males feel especially comfortable and happy with.

In times of stress and crowding there's something very interesting that happens. This is brought out, for example, in the Arnhem colony of chimps in the Netherlands. The males, when they get annoyed, use rocks and stones. They like to throw things. The females are not into missiles. In times of crisis the males can be seen gathering lots of stones—their arms full, their fists clenched—to carry over and throw at their adversaries. The females walk over to these stone-laden males and pry their fingers open, take the stones out, and deposit them on the ground....

I have a feeling that the hereditary predisposition for females as mediators and peacemakers is in the 99.6 percent of the genes we share with the chimps. And that leads me to wonder what the world would be like if women played a role proportionate to their numbers. I don't mean just the occasional woman prime minister who beats the boys at their own game. I mean real, proportionate sharing of power. I mean half, not a few percent, of the members of the Senate—women. I mean half, not zero, of the succession of Presidents being women. I mean half the Joint Chiefs of Staff as women. I mean half of the chief executive officers of major corporations as women.

Maybe it would change nothing. Maybe under these circumstances, the institutions predetermine human behavior, and it doesn't matter whether you're male or female; if you're chairman of the Joint Chiefs of Staff, you have an attitude, and it doesn't matter what brought you to it.

But I like to think that's not the case, that in a world in which women truly share power...we would have a more just, more humane, and more hopeful future. Maybe this is just a pipe dream. But it's a kind of fantasy I couldn't help but have in thinking about this class.

You've been given, in your four years here, some of the tools to preserve and, where necessary, to change the society and the global civilization. No one says this is easy. There are enormous forces of inertia and resistance to any change at all. And there are those who benefit and prosper from there being no change. Nevertheless, it's clear that our civilization is in trouble, that significant changes are necessary. And I hope you will make them.

One of the most important tools is skeptical or critical thinking. Put another way, equip yourself with a baloney detection kit. Because there is an enormous amount of baloney that has to be winnowed out before the few shining gems of truth can be glimpsed. And a lot of that baloney is proffered by those in power. That's their job. Part of the job of education is to be able to tell what's baloney and what's not.

The urgency you feel to make changes is just the extent that change will be made. Don't sit this one out. Don't play it safe. Understand the world, and change it where it needs to be changed. Where it doesn't, leave it alone. Make our society better. Make a world worthy of the children that your generation will bear.

In spite of everything, yes, let's!

VINCENT VAN GOGH

you shall above all things be glad and young

BY E. E. CUMMINGS

you shall above all things be glad and young.
For if you're young,whatever life you wear

it will become you;and if you are glad
whatever's living will yourself become.
Girlboys may nothing more than boygirls need:
i can entirely her only love

whose any mystery makes every man's
flesh put space on;and his mind take off time

that you should ever think,may god forbid
and(in his mercy)your true lover spare:
for that way knowledge lies,the foetal grave
called progress,and negation's dead undoom.

I'd rather learn from one bird how to sing
than teach ten thousand stars how not to dance

MERENGUE, MASSAGE, AND MANGO SORBET: THE ART OF SENSUALITY

"Kama is the enjoyment of appropriate objects by the five senses of hearing, feeling, seeing, tasting and smelling, assisted by the mind together with the soul." —from The Kama Sutra (Aphorisms of Love)

Picture yourself on the beach at sunset. What do you notice? A gentle breeze caresses your face. Cool sand nestles between your toes. Salt air penetrates your nostrils. Rhythmic waves resound in your ears. Striations of lilac and indigo clouds surrounding a blood-orange sun hit your gaze. A warmth flows through you as your partner reaches for your hand. Is this the stuff of a romance novel? Well, maybe it seems a bit "Hollywood" on paper, but it still must strike a cord. You've known moments like this one. Wouldn't it be marvelous to have more of them?

This somewhat cliché beach scenario is filled with sensory delights. But what do you do if the place where you live is landlocked? You can't be running across the country all the time for your sensuality fix. Well, your ability to get the best out of life is intimately tied to your sensory acumen. It is entirely possible to fine-tune your senses and achieve greater awareness of the wonder around you.

Start off by making a list of your favorite things (e.g., chocolate, mango sorbet, foot massages, going to the ballet, outdoor showers, "date night" with your sweetie, playing soccer, the smell in the air after a hard rain, dancing, walking in the woods, art museums, long baths, a vase full of peonies, etc.). Think about what each of your favorites does to your senses. When you soak in the tub, for example, what does it do for your senses? It warms your skin—the largest organ of the body, and therefore the one with the greatest sensory potential. It makes you feel light, and relaxes your muscles. Well, what if you turned it up a notch and transformed your bathroom into a spa? How does a sparkling clean tub of cozy water with bergamot oil sound? Add some candles, your favorite music, a bath pillow, a glass of champagne! Now you've turned the experience into a party for the senses!

You can have greater enjoyment of life simply by paying attention to your experiences and surroundings. The next time you find yourself at an art museum, find a painting or sculpture you are drawn to and really study it. Look at it from far away and up close. Examine the materials and techniques used to create it. Internalize how it makes you feel. Next time you are watching television with your significant other, instead of sitting in close proximity to each other, cuddle. Or, better yet, turn the TV off and give each other a massage. Really feel the warmth of your partner's hands on your skin. Allow yourself to feel the safety and security of your intimacy. Next time you're making dinner, don't just cook—cook with spices! Don't just look at flowers—smell and touch them. Don't just hear music—experience it with your emotions. Trade your flannel pajamas in for some silk ones, or nothing at all. Go skinny-dipping. Look into the eyes of someone you love while they speak—you'll hear better that way! You can truly turn each day into an adventure for the senses.

THE WORLD ACCORDING TO GARP

BY JOHN IRVING

GARP WATCHED WALT, and this calmed him. Garp relished having such close scrutiny of the child; he lay beside Walt and smelled the boy's fresh breath, remembering when Duncan's breath had turned sour in his sleep in that grownup's way. It had been an unpleasant sensation for Garp, shortly after Duncan turned six, to smell that Duncan's breath was stale and faintly foul in his sleep. It was as if the process of decay, of slowly dying, was already begun in him. This was Garp's first awareness of the mortality of his son. There appeared with this odor the first discolorations and stains on Duncan's perfect teeth. Perhaps it was just that Duncan was Garp's firstborn child, but Garp worried more about Duncan than he worried about Walt—even though a five-year-old seems more prone (than a ten-year-old) to the usual childhood accidents. And what are *they*? Garp wondered. Being hit by cars? Choking to death on peanuts? Being stolen by strangers? Cancer, for example, was a stranger.

There was so much to worry about, when worrying about children, and Garp worried so much about everything; at times, especially in these throes of insomnia, Garp thought himself to be psychologically unfit for parenthood. Then he worried about *that*, too, and felt all the more anxious for his children. What if their most dangerous enemy turned out to be *him*?

Author Jack London to His 14-year-old Daughter, Joan

September 16, 1915

Dear Joan:

...Joan, you are on the right track. Never hesitate at making yourself a dainty, delightful girl and woman. There is a girl's pride and a woman's pride in this, and it is indeed a fine pride. On the one hand, of course, never over-dress. On the other hand, never be a frump. No matter how wonderful are the thoughts that burn in your brain, always, physically, and in dress, make yourself a delight to all eyes that behold you.

I have met a number of philosophers. They were real philosophers. Their minds were wonderful minds. But they did not take baths, and they did not change their socks and it almost turned one's stomach to sit at table with them.

Our bodies are as glorious as our minds, and, just as one cannot maintain a high mind in a filthy body, by the same token one cannot keep a high mind and high pride when said body is not dressed beautifully, delightfully, charmingly. Nothing would your Daddy ask better of you in this world than that you have a high mind, a high pride, a find body, and, just as all the rest, a beautifully dressed body.

I do not think you will lose your head. I think, as I read this last letter of yours, that I understand that you have balance, and a woman's balance at that. Never forget the noble things of the spirit, on the other hand, never let your body be ignoble, never let the garmenture of your body be ignoble. As regards the garmenture of your body, learn to do much with little, never to over-do, and to keep such a balance between your garmenture and your mind that both garmenture and mind are beautiful.

I shall not say anything to you about your method of saving, about Bess's method of saving, but there is much I should like to say to you, and, in the meantime I think a lot about it. You are on the right track. Go ahead. Develop your mind to its utmost beauty; and keep your body in pace with your mind.

Daddy

Love After Love

BY DEREK WALCOTT

The time will come
When, with elation,
You will greet yourself arriving
At your own door, in your own mirror,
And each will smile at the other's welcome,

And say, sit here, Eat.
You will love again the stranger who was your self.
Give wine. Give bread. Give back your heart
To itself, to the stranger who has loved you

All your life, whom you ignored
For another, who knows you by heart.
Take down the love letters from the bookshelf,

The photographs, the desperate notes,
Peel your image from the mirror.
Sit. Feast on your life.

There are only two ways to live your life. One is as though nothing is a miracle. The other is as though everything is a miracle.

Albert Einstein

I RECENTLY TURNED FIFTY, which is young for a tree, mid-life for an elephant, and ancient for a quarter-miler, whose son now says, "Dad, I just can't run the quarter with you anymore unless I bring something to read."

Fifty is a nice number for the states in the Union or for a national speed limit, but it is not a number that I was prepared to have hung on *me*. Fifty is supposed to be my *father's* age, but now Bill Cosby, *Junior*, is stuck with these elevated digits and everything they mean. A few days ago, a friend tried to cheer me up by saying, "Fifty is what forty used to be." He had made an inspirational point; and while I ponder it, my forty-year-old knees are suggesting I sit down and my forty-year-old eyes are looking for their glasses, whose location has been forgotten by my forty-year-old mind.

Where To, Old Cos?

BY BILL COSBY

Am I over the hill? They keep telling me that the hill has been moved, that people are younger than ever. And I keep telling *them* that the high-jump bar has dropped from the six feet five I once easily cleared to the four feet nothing that is a Berlin wall for me now. It is not a pretty sight to see a man jumping a tennis net and going down like something snagged by a lobster fisherman.

"You're not getting older, you're getting better," says Dr. Joyce Brothers. This, however, is the kind of doctor who inspires a second opinion.

And so, as I approach the day when my tennis court jumping will be over the balls (or maybe the lines), I am moved to share some thoughts on aging with you, in case you happen to be getting older too. I am moved to reveal how aging feels to me—physically, mentally, and emotionally. Getting older, of course, is a distinctly better change than the one that brings you eulogies. In fact, a poet named Robert Browning considered it the best change of all:

Grow old along with me!
The best is yet to be.

On the days when I need aspirin to get out of bed, Browning is clearly a minor poet; but he was an optimist and there is always comfort in his lines, no matter how much you ache.

Whether or not Browning was right, most of my first fifty years have been golden ones. I have been an exceedingly lucky man, so I will settle for what is ahead being as good as what has gone by. I find myself moving toward what is ahead with a curious blend of both fighting and accepting the aging of Cosby, hoping that the philosopher was right when he said, "Old is always fifteen years from now."

Turning fifty has not bothered me, but people keep saying it *should* have, for fifty is one of those milestone ages that end in zero. Of course, in America *every* age ending in zero is considered a milestone age. Fifty is called the Big Five-O, but Forty is The Big Four-O and Thirty is The Big Three-O. A few months ago, my youngest daughter hit the Big One-O and she wasn't happy about it.

"I wish there were more single figures," she said.

Although reaching this half-century mark has not traumatized me, it *has* left me with disbelief about the flight of time. It seems that only yesterday I was fifteen and old people were people of forty, who were always going someplace to sit down. And now *I* am doing the sitting; and now my wife is telling me,"You *sit* too much. You should get up and *do* something."

"Okay," I say, "let's have some sex."

"Just *sit* there."

When I was eight, an uncle said, "Bill, how long would you like to live?"

"A hundred million years," I replied.

"That's a ripe old age. I wonder what you'll *look* like at a hundred million."

"Oh, I'll just be me," I said.

Now, however, considerably short of the hundred-million mark, I am having to learn to accept a new me, one who has to drink skim milk, which looks like the wash for a paintbrush; one whose stomach refuses to process another jalapeño pepper; and one for whom a lobster is crustacean cyanide.

"If you want a lobster," my doctor says, "just eat the shell."

Have I *also* become just the shell? Well, in one or two places, the meat *is* missing. For example, I am now a man with the ability to dial a telephone number and, while the phone is ringing, forget whom he is calling. Just yesterday, I made such a blind call and a person answered with a voice I did not know. Like a burglar doing research, I quickly hung up, and then I thought about age.

Wiser men than I have thought about age and have never figured out anything to do except say, "Happy birthday." What, after all, *is* old? To a child of seven, ten is old; and to a child of ten, twenty-five is middle-aged and fifty is an archaeological exhibit. And to me, a man of seventy is... what I want to be, weighing 195, playing tennis with convalescents, and hearing well enough to hear one of my grandchildren sweetly say, "Grandpa, was 'The Cosby Show' anything like 'I Love Lucy'?"

THE MOTH AND THE STAR

BY JAMES THURBER

A YOUNG AND IMPRESSIONABLE moth once set his heart on a certain star. He told his mother about this and she counseled him to set his heart on a bridge lamp instead. "Stars aren't the thing to hang around," she said; "lamps are the thing to hang around." "You get somewhere that way," said the moth's father. "You don't get anywhere chasing stars." But the moth would not heed the words of either parent. Every evening at dusk when the star came out he would start flying toward it and every morning at dawn he would crawl back home worn out with his vain endeavor. One day his father said to him, "You haven't burned a wing in months, boy, and it looks to me as if you were never going to. All your brothers have been badly burned flying around street lamps and all your sisters have been terribly singed flying around house

lamps. Come on, now, get out of here and get yourself scorched! A big strapping moth like you without a mark on him!"

The moth left his father's house, but he would not fly around street lamps and he would not fly around house lamps. He went right on trying to reach the star, which was four and one-third light years, or twenty-five trillion miles, away. The moth thought it was just caught in the top branches of an elm. He never did reach the star, but he went right on trying, night after night, and when he was a very, very old moth he began to think that he really had reached the star and he went around saying so. This gave him a deep and lasting pleasure, and he lived to a great old age. His parents and his brothers and his sisters had all been burned to death when they were quite young.

Moral: *Who flies afar from the sphere of our sorrow is here today and here tomorrow.*

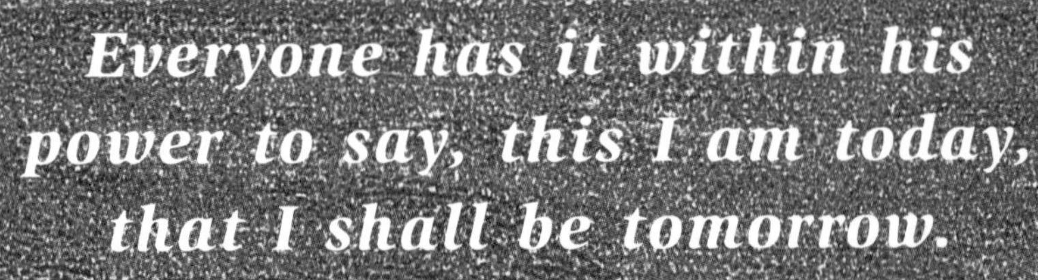

Everyone has it within his power to say, this I am today, that I shall be tomorrow.

Louis L'Amour

The Glory of Love

BY BILLY HILL

You've got to give a little, take a little
And let your poor heart break a little,
That's the story of,
That's the glory of love,

You've got to laugh a little, cry a little
Before the clouds roll by a little
That's the story of,
That's the glory of love.

As long as there's the two of us
We've got the world and all its charms
And when the world is through with us
We've got each other's arms
You've got to win a little, lose a little
And always have the blues a little
That's the story of,
That's the glory of love.

To laugh often and much, to win the respect of intelligent people and the affection of children; to earn the appreciation of honest critics and endure the betrayal of false friends; to appreciate beauty; to find the best in others; to leave the world a bit better, whether by a healthy child, a garden patch or a redeemed social condition; to know even one life has breathed easier because you have lived. This is to have succeeded.

RALPH WALDO EMERSON

MADELEINE ALBRIGHT

MOUNT HOLYOKE COLLEGE
MAY 25, 1997

...AS INDIVIDUALS EACH OF US MUST CHOOSE whether to live our lives narrowly, selfishly, and complacently or to act with courage and faith.

As a nation America must choose whether to turn inward and betray the lessons of history or to seize the opportunity before us to shape history....

The Berlin Wall is now a memory. We could be satisfied with that. Instead we are enlarging and adapting NATO and striving to create a future for Europe in which every democracy—including Russia—is our partner and every partner is a builder of peace.

Largely because of U.S. leadership, nuclear weapons no longer target our homes. We could relax. Instead we are working to reduce nuclear arsenals further, eliminate chemical weapons, end the child-maiming scourge of land mines, and ratify a treaty that would ban nuclear explosions forever....

We have built a growing world economy in which those with modern skills and available capital have done very well. We could stop there. Instead we are pursuing a broader prosperity, in which those entrapped by poverty and discrimination are empowered to share and in which every democracy on every continent will be included.

In our lifetimes we have seen enormous advances in the status of women. We could now lower our

voices and—as some suggest—sit sedately down. Instead women everywhere—whether bumping against a glass ceiling or rising from a dirt floor—are standing up, spreading the word that we are ready to claim our rightful place as full citizens and full participants in every society on earth.

Mount Holyoke is the home, to borrow Wendy Wasserstein's phrase, of "uncommon women." But we know that there are uncommon women in all corners of the globe.

In recent years I have met in Sarajevo with women weighted down by personal grief reaching out across ethnic lines to rebuild their shattered society.

In Burundi I have seen women taking the lead in efforts to avoid the fate of neighboring Rwanda, where violence left three quarters of the population female, and one half of the women widows.

In Guatemala I have talked to women striving to ensure that their new peace endures and is accompanied by justice and an end to discrimination and abuse.

And in Burma I have met with a remarkable woman named Aung San Suu Kyi, who risks her life every day to keep alive the hope for democracy in her country.

These women have in common a determination to chart their own path and, by so doing, to alter for the better the course of their country or community.

Each has suffered blows, but each has proceeded with courage. Each has persevered.

As you go along your own road in life, you will, if you aim high enough, also meet resistance, for as Robert Kennedy once said, "If there's nobody in your way, it's because you're not going anywhere." But no matter how tough the opposition may seem, have courage still—and persevere.

There is no doubt, if you aim high your efforts to change the world or improve the lot of those around you do not mean much in the grand scheme of things But no matter how impotent you may sometimes feel, have courage still—and persevere.

It is certain, if you aim high enough, that you will find your strongest beliefs ridiculed and challenged; principles that you cherish may be derisively dismissed by those claiming to be more practical or realistic than you. But no matter how weary you may become in persuading others to see the value in what you value, have courage still—and persevere.

Inevitably, if you aim high enough, you will be buffeted by demands of family, friends, and employment that will conspire to distract you from your course. But no matter how difficult it may be to meet the commitments you have made, have courage still—and persevere.

It has been said that all work that is worth anything is done in faith.

This morning, in these beautiful surroundings, at this celebration of warm memory and high expectation, I summon you in the name of this historic college and of all who have passed through its halls, to embrace the faith that your courage and your perseverance will make a difference and that every life enriched by your giving, every friend touched by your affection, every soul inspired by your passion, and every barrier to justice brought down by your determination will ennoble your own life, inspire others, serve your country, and explode outward the boundaries of what is achievable on this earth.

From CAT'S CRADLE

By Kurt Vonnegut

"He was supposed to be our commencement speaker," said Sandra.

"Who was?" I asked.

"Dr. Hoenikker—the old man."

"What did he say?"

"He didn't show up."

"So you didn't get a commencement address?"

"Oh, we got one. Dr. Breed, the one you're gonna see tomorrow, he showed up, all out of breath, and he gave some kind of talk."

"What did he say?"

"He said he hoped a lot of us would have careers in science," she said. She didn't see anything funny in that. She was remembering a lesson that had impressed her. She was repeating it gropingly, dutifully. "He said, the trouble with the world was . . ."

She had to stop and think.

"The trouble with the world was," she continued hesitatingly, "that people were still superstitious instead of scientific. He said if everybody would study science more, there wouldn't be all the trouble there was."

"He said science was going to discover the basic secret of life someday," the bartender put in. He scratched his head and frowned. "Didn't I read in the paper the other day where they'd finally found out what it was?"

"I missed that," I murmured.

"I saw that," said Sandra. "About two days ago."

"That's right," said the bartender.

"What *is* the secret of life?" I asked.

"I forget," said Sandra.

"Protein," the bartender declared. "They found out something about protein."

"Yeah," said Sandra, "that's it."

To me, if life boils down to one significant thing, it's movement. To live is to keep moving. Unfortunately, this means that for the rest of our lives we're going to be looking for boxes.

When you're moving, your whole world is boxes. That's all you think about. "Boxes, where are there boxes?" You just wander down the street going in and out of stores, "Are there boxes here? Have you seen any boxes?" It's all you think about. You can't even talk to people, you can't concentrate. "Will you shut up? I'm looking for boxes!"

Homestretch

BY JERRY SEINFELD

After a while, you become like a bloodhound on the scent. You walk into a store, "There's boxes here. Don't tell me you don't have boxes, dammit, I can smell 'em!" I become obsessed. "I love the smell of cardboard in the morning." You could be at a funeral, everyone's mourning, crying around you, you're looking at the casket. "That's a nice box. Does anybody know where that guy got that box? When he's done with it, you think I could get that? It's got some nice handles on it. My stereo would fit right in there."

I mean that's what death is, really, it's the last big move of your life. The hearse is like the van, the pallbearers are your close friends, the only ones you could really ask to help you with a big move like that. And the casket is that great, perfect box you've been looking for your whole life. The only problem is once you find it, you're in it.

Ode To My Socks

BY PABLO NERUDA

Maru Mori brought me
a pair
of socks
which she knitted with her
own
sheepherder hands,
two socks as soft
as rabbits.
I slipped my feet
into them
as if they were
two
cases
knitted
with threads of
twilight
and the pelt of sheep.

Outrageous socks,
my feet became
two fish
made of wool,
two long sharks
of ultramarine blue
crossed
by one golden hair,
two gigantic blackbirds,
two cannons:
my feet
were honored in this way
by
these
heavenly
socks.
They were
so beautiful
that for the first time
my feet seemed to me
unacceptable
like two decrepit
firemen, firemen
unworthy

of that embroidered
fire,
of those luminous
socks.

Nevertheless,
I resisted
the sharp temptation
to save them
as schoolboys
keep fireflies,
as scholars
collect
sacred documents,
I resisted
the wild impulse
to put them
in a golden
cage
and each day give them
birdseed
and chunks of pink melon.
Like explorers
in the jungle
who hand over the rare
green deer
to the roasting spit
and eat it
with remorse,
I stretched out
my feet
and pulled on
the
magnificent
socks
and
then my shoes.

And the moral of my ode
it this:
beauty is twice
beauty
and what is good is doubly
good
when it's a matter of two
woolen socks
in winter.

If you fall, boy, you don't have to wallow. Ain't nobody going to think you somebody unless you think so yourself. Don't listen to their talk, boy, they don't have a pot to pee in or a window to throw it out. For God's sake, Jesse, promise me you'll be somebody. Ain't no such thing as "cain't," "cain't" got drowned in a soda bottle. Don't let the Joneses get you down. Nothing is impossible for those who love the Lord. Come hell or high water, if you got guts, boy, ain't nothing nobody can turn you around.

MATILDA BURNS,
JESSE JACKSON'S GRANDMOTHER

Father and Son

WORDS AND MUSIC BY CAT STEVENS

I was once like you are now
And I know that it's not easy
To be calm when you've found
Something going on.
But take your time, think a lot.
I think of everything you've got.
For you will still be here tomorrow
But your dreams may not.

(Chorus)
It's not time to make a change
Just relax, take it easy.
You're still young, that's your fault
There's so much you have to know.
Find a girl, settle down.
If you want you can marry.
Look at me,
I am old but I'm happy

How can I try to explain?
When I do he turns away again.
It's always been the same, same old
story.
From the moment I could talk
I was ordered to listen
Now there's a way and I know
That I have to go away,
I know I have to go.

(Chorus)

All the times that I've cried
Keepin' all the things I knew inside.
It's hard, but it's harder
To ignore it.
If they were right I'd agree
But it's them they know, not me.
Now there's a way and I know
That I have to go away.
I know I have to go.

Nothing Gold Can Stay

BY ROBERT FROST

Nature's first green is gold,

Her hardest hue to hold.

Her early leaf's a flower;

But only so an hour.

Then leaf subsides to leaf.

So Eden sank to grief,

So dawn goes down to day.

Nothing gold can stay.

Light tomorrow with today.

ELIZABETH BARRETT BROWNING

KEEPING A DREAM JOURNAL

Dreams are the touchstones of our character. —Henry David Thoreau

WHAT ARE DREAMS?

We humans have been eternally fascinated by our dreams. The ancient Greeks believed they were visionary stories relayed by the gods. It wasn't until the 5th century B.C.E. that Plato challenged the concept of the prophetic dream. He understood dreams as nothing other than the inner workings of the dreamer's mind. The Bible revived the notion of supernaturally influenced dreams—the most famous of which was given to Jacob, who dreamed of a ladder stretching from Earth into heaven.

Modern dream theories tend to agree with Plato. Carl Jung (1875–1961), a pupil of Sigmund Freud (1856–1939), saw dreams as the vehicle through which the unconscious mind speaks to the conscious mind. He believed that only through careful study of and reflection on our own dreams might we gain a sense of contentment and completeness.

"The images of the unconscious place a great responsibility upon a man. Failure to understand them...deprives him of his wholeness and imposes a painful fragmentariness on his life."

WHY DO YOU DREAM?

During the course of an average day, you spend 16–18 hours taking in external stimuli. Your brain continually receives more information than you can readily assimilate into your consciousness. That's where dreams come in. When you sleep, your mind is still hard at work—it sorts through all the images and ideas you were unable to consciously act upon throughout the day, and adds to them unresolved issues from the past. The ideas that are floating around in your subconscious mind find their way into your dreams. Since the logic of the unconscious mind is often mysterious, the images you are shown in your dreams rarely have a basis in reality. More frequently, these images are symbols that you must attempt to interpret according to your own unique experience. No one else can assign meaning to the symbols of your dreams. Your dreams are about you, and therefore you are the one person supremely qualified to interpret them.

WHAT ARE YOUR DREAMS TRYING TO TELL YOU?

What secrets do you think your unconscious mind is trying to tell you? Is the key to unlocking your happiness hidden in your dreams? One way to tap into your subconscious is by keeping a dream journal. Successful integration of your conscious and subconscious mind is hard work, but it is work that can provide you with the tools necessary to become a happier, more whole person. The powerful process of keeping a journal will allow you to see inside yourself more clearly than you ever have. Here's how to start the dialog with your subconscious:

Before you write a word, it's a good idea to practice dream recall. Approach this as a skill. Before you go to sleep, tell yourself that you will remember your dreams. Don't get discouraged if it doesn't happen right away. It may take a week or so to establish the habit, and even then you may not recall your dreams every day. If you have trouble, try to read books about dreams before bed. Meditate or pray about dreaming. Research dream symbols.

Once you've established the habit of recalling your dreams, it is time to start recording. Your journal can be anything from a notepad to a handmade book.

Each night before bed, review the previous few dreams you recorded in your journal. Next, write the date on a new page, and write a sentence or two about your day—exciting events, goals you are working toward at home or at work, things that may have upset you, etc. This will help achieve the right frame of mind for linking your conscious and subconscious. As you have been doing with the recall practice, tell yourself you want to remember your dreams and engage with your subconscious.

Keep your journal and pen by your bedside (with a flashlight if you wish). If you wake in the night with a dream memory, jot it down.

When you wake up in the morning, whatever you do, DON'T GET OUT OF BED! First, write anything you remember about your dreams in your journal. Even if you don't remember your whole dream, write down what you do remember. Sometimes key words or images are all that you need to help interpret your dream. You may find it helpful to write out what comes to you with codes and shorthand. An example of a code may be placing a small question mark next to a fuzzy detail that you intend to fill in later. Once you have the broad picture down on paper, you can go back and fill in the details as they come to you. Bits and pieces may be all you recall at first. Your dreams should become more and more lucid with time.

Look over your entry and think about what events may have triggered that particular dream. Write down any connections or interpretations of symbols that come to you.

Carry your journal with you, or a smaller notepad, so you can write down anything you remember during the course of the day. Also, be sure to record when and where the memory came to your attention. This may help you figure out what triggered the memory and evaluate whether or not it plays a role in the dream interpretation.

After several weeks of establishing this habit, you may discover that you are having an easier time recalling your dreams, and that they are more lucid. You may even be an active participant in your dreams. There are ways to encourage more lucid dreaming. Try to remember what you were doing over the past few hours. If you are dreaming, you won't be able to, or it will be illogical, even to your subconscious. Or, you can try to jump up and fly within your dream. Try breathing into your hand or moving or manipulating something with your mind. These tricks generally help you to be able to participate in your dreams and to better remember them in the morning.

You may notice recurring dreams or symbols in your dreams. Pay close attention to these dreams as they are usually an indication that your subconscious is desperately trying to tell you something.

What you do with all the information you compile is up to you. But close observation of the patterns and symbols of your dreams can help you to deal with your fears, inhibitions, insecurities, and other problems. The more you engage with your dreams and act upon what they are trying to tell you, the more self-aware and fulfilled you will be.

Sweet dreams!

Hold Fast Your Dreams

LOUISE DRISCOLL

Hold fast your dreams!
Within your heart
Keep one still, secret spot
Where dreams may go,
And, sheltered so,
May thrive and grow
Where doubt and fear are not.
Oh keep a place apart,
Within your heart,
For little dreams to go!

Think still of lovely things that are not true.
Let wish and magic work at will in you.
Be sometimes blind to sorrow. Make believe!
Forget the calm that lies
In disillusioned eyes.
Though we all know that we must die,
Yet you and I
May walk like gods and be
Even now at home in immortality.

We see so many ugly things—
Deceits and wrongs and quarrelings;
We know, Alas! we know
How quickly fade
The color in the west,
The bloom upon the flower,
The bloom upon the breast
And youth's blind hour.
Yet keep within your heart
A place apart
Where little dreams may go,
May thrive and grow.
Hold fast—hold fast your dreams!

CORINTHIANS 13: 6-13

NEW TESTAMENT, KING JAMES BIBLE

REJOICETH NOT IN INIQUITY, but rejoiceth in the truth;

Beareth all things, believeth all things, hopeth all things, endureth all things.

Charity never falleth: but whether *there be* prophecies, they shall fail: whether *there be* tongues, they shall cease; whether *there be* knowledge, it shall vanish away.

For we know in part, and we prophesy in part.

But when that which is perfect is come, then that which is in part shall be done away.

When I was a child, I spake as a child, I understood as a child, I thought as a child: but when I became a man, I put away childish things.

For now we see through a glass, darkly; but then face to face: now I know in part; but then shall I know even as also I am known.

And now abideth faith, hope, charity, these three; but the greatest of these *is* charity.

M · P

There will come a time when you believe everything is finished. That will be the beginning.

Louis L'Amour

ILLUSTRATION CREDITS: Cover, pgs. 35, 47, 62, 98, 185, 188, 244: Jessie Wilcox Smith. Pgs. and 349 Maxfield Parrish ®/Licensed by AsaP and VAGA, New York, NY. Pgs. 10-11, 60, 23 294-295, 316-317: S. Barham. Pg. 12: C.H. Pless. Pg. 17: Simon Thomas. Pg. 32: Tenggren. P 50-51: Bernhardt Wall. Pgs. 52, 286: H.Y. Hintermeister. Pg. 106: Paul Bramsom. Pg.115: M Musselman. Pgs. 118, 334, 351: Miriam Story Hurford. Pgs.120-121, 327: Benjamin Rolbi Pg. 135: Nina B. Mason. Pg.159: Vernon Thomas. Pgs. 162-163: L. Perrault. Pg. 174: Juli Barret Mansfield. Pg. 182: Maud Humphreys. Pg. 199: Starmer. Pg. 217: J. Knowles Ha Pgs. 224-225: Janet Laura Scott. Pg. 226: Raymond Thayer. Pg. 253: C.H. Twelvetrees. Pg. 25 Ellen H. Clapsaddle. Pg. 259: Margaret Meade Price. Pg. 261: Ethel Parkinson. Pg. 290: Laws Wood. Pg. 318: Gen Davis. Pg. 328: R.F. Outcault.